PUMPERS
WORKHORSE
FIRE ENGINES

Larry Shapiro

MBI Publishing Company

First published in 1999 by MBI Publishing Company, 729 Prospect Avenue, PO Box 1, Osceola, WI 54020-0001 USA.

The information in this book is true and complete to the best of our knowledge. All recommendations are made without any guarantee on the part of the author or Publisher, who also disclaim any liability incurred in connection with the use of this data or specific details.

We recognize that some words, model names, and designations, for example, mentioned herein are the property of the trademark holder. We use them for identification purposes only. This is not an official publication.

MBI Publishing Company books are also available at discounts in bulk quantity for industrial or sales-promotional use. For details write to Special Sales Manager at the Motorbooks International Wholesalers & Distributors, 729 Prospect Avenue, PO Box 1, Osceola, WI 54020-0001 USA.

Library of Congress Cataloging-in-Publication Data
    Shapiro, Larry
    Pumpers: Workhorse Fire Engines / Larry Shapiro
       p. cm.
    Includes index.
    ISBN 0-7603-0672-9 (pbk. : alk. paper)
    1. Fire engines--History. 2. Fire pumps--History.
    I. Title.
TH9371.S464 1999
628.9'259--dc21   99-37654

On the front cover: The Fowlerville, Michigan, Fire Department drafts from a portable tank with its 1998 Pierce Quantum pumper. The front intake port has a swivel feature to allow the preconnected hard suction hose to drop right into the portable tank for quick drafting operations.

On the frontispiece: The deck gun is being used from this Pierce Arrow pumper in an attempt to extinguish this smoky fire in a commercial block of stores. Early models of the Arrow featured a front door and door jam that was straight instead of curved.

On the title page: The Billingsport Fire Association of Paulsboro, New Jersey, owns this 1955 Mack Model B85F-1082 pumper. It carries 400 gallons of water and has a 750-gallon per minute pump. The orange flashlight and modern fire extinguishers were not assigned to the original unit. Note the storage of boots to accommodate volunteers, who would meet the pumper at the fire scene.

On the back cover: Top-San Francisco purchased several of these 1,500-gallon per minute pumpers in 1985. Built by SPI on Kenworth L700 Series chassis, they were modified with a crew enclosure that had a raised roof. The tight turning radius was important, as illustrated on this sharp curve. Bottom-A Pierce Lance pumper with a 20-inch raised roof sits in an alley, running several attack lines that are tangled in the street.

Edited by Mike Haenggi
Designed by Dan Perry

Printed in Hong Kong

CONTENTS

	Acknowledgments	6
	Introduction	7
CHAPTER 1	A Brief Overview of the Modern Pumper	9
CHAPTER 2	Pumper Manufacturers, Big and Small	13
CHAPTER 3	Pumper Design	51
CHAPTER 4	Trucks and Firefighters in Action	71
CHAPTER 5	The Manufacturers of Today	85
CHAPTER 6	Pumpers for the Future	123
	Index	127

ACKNOWLEDGMENTS

This book has a tremendous amount of information pertaining to the modern progression of pumpers in the fire service. Much of it is information I have amassed in the many years that I have been involved with the fire service. Although I worked diligently to ensure complete accuracy while writing this book, I cannot say with absolute certainty that I did not overlook some points or perhaps attribute something to the wrong year. Rest assured that to the best of my ability, the book is thorough, accurate, and complete. In addition, many individuals spent their time checking, correcting, and supplying the information that is included here. I wish to mention everyone here, though I will undoubtedly omit someone. To those who find themselves overlooked, please forgive me.

Listed alphabetically, my thanks and appreciation go out to the following people: Jim Bodony, Mid-America Truck and Equipment Company; Bob Barraclough, Class 1; J. T. Duke, Fire and Rescue Apparatus; Bill Foster, Spartan Motors, Inc.; Captain Don Freuser, Los Angeles City Fire Department; Sonya Gossett, E-One; Rob Haldeman, Ladder Towers, Inc.; Ben Hoppe, FWD Seagrave Corporation; Ken Lenz, HME, Inc.; Captain Dennis Moon and the C-Shift, San Bernardino City, California; Captain Craig Moore, Glendale, California; Steve Morelli, Freightliner Trucks; Roger Parker, Luverne Fire Apparatus; Glen Prezembel, Mid-America Truck and Equipment Company; Greg Shantz, Shantz and Company; Kirsten Skyba and Barbara Weber, Pierce Manufacturing.

There are a tremendous number of words in this book, and my wife, Dorothy, diligently read each and every one several times. Realizing that much of the text might be considered dry reading to someone who does not share a passion for the fire service, I owe her an untold amount of gratitude, along with the promise that I will not pursue too many more titles with this format.

As a fire buff, enthusiast, and collector, I have long been a stickler for the little details that separate the rigs by model years and enhancements. What year did a manufacturer change the grille design or the door style? I've always wondered why model names or numbers were not used consistently by some companies, while others were diligent in providing cohesive documentation for every change and improvement. I hope the pages that follow provide the explanations to those who share my compulsive tendencies, and provide some answers to the nagging questions concerning the evolution of modern pumpers.

Should any experts, authorities, or otherwise knowledgeable people in the field find any mistakes, I would welcome the corrections in order to update future revisions of this book or subsequent ones.

I would like to dedicate this book to four men who are no longer with us. I met each of them through my experiences in the fire service and have the pleasure of knowing that each enriched my life. I had the benefit of learning from them and sharing with them my love for the fire service. I will miss them.

In memory of
  Roger Coulter
  Wayne Luecht
  Ron Mattes
  Larry McGlaughlin

INTRODUCTION

The mainstay of the fire industry is the pumper. This is the vehicle commonly referred to as a fire truck or a fire engine. Along with ladder trucks, the pumper is the most recognizable piece of fire apparatus, and that which is found in the largest number. Every fire department has at least one pumper. Most have several. The ratio of pumpers to ladder trucks is at least three or four to one.

Pumpers first came into existence with the horse-drawn steam pumpers of the 1800s, followed by the introduction of gasoline-powered vehicles in the early 1900s. This book will not dive into the historical origin of the antique units, which is worthy of an entire volume of works. Instead, the discussion here will begin with a more modern era, emphasizing the years from the 1960s through the current day and ending with a brief look into the years to come. It would not be possible to represent every company that has built pumpers during this timeframe since there have been and continue to be many small "mom and pop" companies that turn out less than 10 units in a calendar year. I hope, with few exceptions, this book will illustrate a broad sample of the types, styles, companies, and unique units that have protected citizens around the country during this modern time period.

It will also serve to provide explanations of various models and styles produced by the major builders with a chronology of changes and improvements. The evolution of cab and chassis styles with the yearly upgrades will be outlined, including those that were introduced to meet regulatory criteria, as well as the industry innovations that came from each manufacturer.

Chapter 1 begins with a quick glance at the early years of modern fire apparatus. A few shots depict some of the styles from the 1920s, 1930s, and through to the 1960s.

Chapter 2 shows commercial and custom units from the major players in the industry during the modern era, 1970 through 1980, along with units from small regional builders. Pumpers are featured from departments throughout the country. Big cities like New York, Chicago, Boston, and Los Angeles are highlighted, as well as towns on Long Island, in Wisconsin, and those from many other states on both coasts.

Chapter 3 is dedicated to describing all aspects of constructing a pumper, and changes that have occurred in the production of units, both in terms of safety and technological improvements. Chassis, cabs, pumps, tanks, body styles, building materials, gauges, and the equipment carried is discussed.

Chapter 4 illustrates how the pumpers are operated, and their deployment in the field. Run-of-the-mill situations are covered, as are the big jobs.

Chapter 5 displays the units that are made today. Builders featured include American LaFrance, Central States, Darley, E-ONE, HME, Luverne, Pierce, Quality, Seagrave, Smeal, Spartan, Sutphen, 3D, and many smaller regional companies.

Chapter 6 explores actual and theoretical concepts to take the pumper into the twenty-first century and beyond. Changes in construction techniques, building materials, and basic designs are illustrated through photographs and drawings. Some companies have already begun construction of these units, while others remain in the design stage, constantly updating the products before they are built.

CHAPTER 1
A Brief Overview of the Modern Pumper

Long after motorized fire apparatus was commonplace, each of the prominent companies that produced these vehicles had its own proprietary designs and styles. Names like American LaFrance, FWD, Mack, Pirsch, and Seagrave produced units that were easily distinguished from the others, and these led the market from 1940 to the mid-1960s. Although many fire engines had open cab designs with no roof, most companies were moving toward variations that offered an enclosed cab for some of the crewmembers. Firefighters commonly rode on the rear tailboard of the apparatus while holding on. Often only the driver and officer sat in the cab.

World War II affected the fire service in many ways. First and foremost, fire apparatus production was at a virtual standstill, as manufacturers switched their plants to wartime efforts. Raw materials too were directed toward the war effort.

American LaFrance introduced the first cab-forward design with the 700 Series. Here a refurbished 1956 pumper from Batavia, Illinois, is shown with ground ladders mounted on the driver's side that extend above the pump panel. This rig has a 1000-gpm pump and carries 500 gallons of water.

9

This is a 1949 FWD sedan cab pumper with a 500-gpm pump and a 750-gallon water tank. Ladder storage is both overhead and on the officer's side. Behind the cab is a booster reel.

A conventional-design pumper from Peter Pirsch and Sons of Kenosha, Wisconsin, sits at a fire scene in Morton Grove, Illinois. This 1956 pumper carried 500 gallons of water that supplied a 1000-gpm pump. The sedan cab accommodated two, so the other firefighters had to ride the tailboard.

After the war ended, the fire service began to use two-way radios for dispatch and communication. High-pressure fog pumpers were developed after learning from the U.S. Navy's use of them to combat shipboard fires. The biggest effect from the ending of the war was the enormous surge in fire apparatus production to update fleets that had been neglected for several years.

This period also saw the introduction of the diesel engine as an alternative to the gasoline-powered engines that were standard for all fire trucks. Power steering and automatic transmissions soon followed.

In the mid-1940s, American LaFrance was ahead of the times in introducing the 700 Series, the first cab-forward design for fire trucks. FWD and Pirsch both built conventional styles with the engine ahead of the cab. Seagrave produced the conventional B Series, and Mack had both the L Model and the B Model, which were also conventional designs. It wasn't until the late 1950s that Mack, Maxim, and Seagrave began to build their cab-forward, fixed-cab designs. At the same time, International and Ford introduced commercial tilt-cab chassis. The Ford C-Series would go on to become the most popular commercial chassis to be used in the fire service. This was a major change in the appearance and construction of fire trucks.

Other cab-forward designs followed in the early 1960s, from Crown, Duplex, Hahn, Pirsch, and Ward LaFrance. Oshkosh, Sutphen, and Young began producing cab-forward designs in the late 1960s, and in the early 1970s, two companies, Hendrickson and Imperial, began producing custom cab-forward chassis available to any body builder that did not make its own.

A 1952 open-cab Seagrave 531-B pumper with a 750-gpm pump and 300-gallon water tank. Ground ladder storage is on an overhead rack. At the time of this photo, the fire department had mounted a modern lightbar above the ladder rack.

CHAPTER 2
Pumper Manufacturers, Big and Small

During the years between 1970 and 1990, pumper design and manufacture saw many changes. More than 30 companies producing pumpers began to carve out niches through the design elements they were using. Cab-forward designs were now the predominant style, and it became necessary to improve on these designs and introduce new options that would change the look of units to come. One new start-up company called Emergency One began in Ocala, Florida, in 1974, and would go on to become one of the major fire truck producers in the world.

The big names at that time were American LaFrance, Emergency One, FMC, Grumman, Mack, Pirsch, Pierce, Seagrave, and Ward LaFrance. Other companies building pumpers during this period included Alexis, American, American Eagle, Boardman, Boyer, Crown, Darley, Ferrara, 4 Guys, Hahn, Indiana Fire Apparatus, KME, Maxim, Quality, Saulsbury, Steeldraulics, Sutphen, Van Pelt, Ward '79, Western States, and Young.

Changes during the late 1970s into the 1980s started with the widening of cabs from the standard 86 inches to 94 inches with fenders becoming recessed into the cab. Several companies that were building their own cabs from scratch decided to

The Shrewesbury Fire Company in Pennsylvania is a loyal Spartan customer with three matching Gladiator chassis in its barn.

13

A 1986 National Foam pumper for Greensboro, North Carolina, with a Duplex D350 cab.

The Custom Chassis Makers
Duplex

Duplex, a custom chassis builder located in Ohio, offered several cab and chassis styles based on TCM cabs. Duplex models during the 1970s were the R-300 curved windshield, and the R-200 flat windshield, 84-inch narrow-cab styles. This was a carryover from the period when the Warner-Swassey Company owned it. Duplex was later sold to the Nolan Company. It continued to offer stationary cab designs. The D-250, a model with an 84-inch-wide, cab flat-windshield, and squared-front was produced in the early 1980s. The D-250-T version featured a tandem rear axle for pumper-tankers and aerials. Duplex offered two cab styles with curved windshields and rounded features. The D-400 series was designed for aerials with a low-profile, 84-inch-wide cab and tandem rear axles. The D-300 series for pumpers offered a conventional height, low profile (D-300-LP) and four-door (D-300-FD) version. This was also an 84-inch-wide style and like the other available models, was a stationary-cab design. In the mid-1980s, Duplex widened all of its cab styles to 94 inches. Model numbers changed at this time. The D-300 rounded series became the D-350 Enforcer, which was available in a two-door canopy cab or a four-door enclosed crew cab. The two-door canopy cab featured two, rear-facing seats, one on either side of the engine housing. The D-250 became the D-260 Liberty series, and the D-400 was now the D-450 Defender low-profile series, that again was primarily an aerial chassis.

capitalize on another company that was mass producing cabs for others. As a result, Pirsch, for instance, discontinued its trademark cab design in favor of the simpler contour cab manufactured by Truck Cab Manufacturers (TCM) of Cincinnati, Ohio. American, Boardman, Duplex, Hendrickson, Imperial (later purchased by and called Pemfab), Oshkosh, Spartan, and Ward '79 also used this cab, which came to be referred to as the Cincinnati Cab.

TCM offered several styles, and could also customize a proprietary design for individual companies. Several of these designs were for custom chassis builders. Pemfab had a unique style that it called the wedge. The front of the cab, from the bumper line to the cab's roof, was angled in a straight line. Spartan purchased a squared cab style that was called the CFG model, and a unique version that combined both squared and contoured designs, known as the CFV or Maxi-Vision. Hendrickson had its 1871-S squared-front cab, which was the standard for custom fire trucks built for many years until it was replaced by the 1871-W. Pierce and Emergency One used these styles quite extensively until they began to produce their own cabs that did not originate from TCM.

Chassis Jargon	
ER	Emergency Rescue
LFD	Long Four-Door
LFDSC	Long Four-Door Super Command
LMFD	Long Medium Four-Door
LMFDSC	Long Medium Four-Door Super Command
MFD	Medium Four-Door
MFDSC	Medium Four-Door Super Command
SFD	Short Four-Foor
SMFD	Short Medium Four-Door
SMFDSC	Short Medium Four-Door Super Command

The standard engine for the D-350 and the D-260 was the 320-horsepower, six-cylinder, Detroit Diesel 6V-92TA. Matched with that was the Spicer 1252-A transmission. Similar to the other chassis builders, optional engines were available with up to 475 horsepower and eight cylinders. These chassis models were available through the 1980s and into early 1990s. In 1987, Duplex introduced a tilt-cab model, the D-500 Vanguard, a split tilt design. The cab split over the front axle with the rear section remaining in place, while the front tilted for access to the engine. This design required an Allison automatic transmission and offered a 40-degree cramp angle for a short turning radius, the industry unit of measure. For the first time, Duplex now offered an expansive list of cab options for the Vanguard, including the standard two-door canopy cab, a two-door model with a sliding rear enclosure (SFD), a standard four-door design (MFD), as well as a short four-door design (SMFD), and a raised roof four-door version(MFDR). Shortly after the Vanguard was introduced, Simon, a

European company, bought Duplex. The Liberty was removed from the product line-up, but the Enforcer, Defender, and Vanguard remained in place for several years.

In the early 1990s, Simon-Duplex began reworking its cab styles, leading to the D8400 Classic and Mark II series, as well as the D9400 and D9500 Signature series. The two series shared the same cab with one difference. The D9400 and D9500 cabs had a full-length door where the step was enclosed. The D8400 cabs had a shorter door with an exposed step. Both of these styles were available with a full range of cab configurations. Offering the newest Detroit Diesel Series 60 and the Cummins N14 engines with outputs of 500 horsepower, these new full tilt-cab models were very popular. The largest designs provided seating for a maximum of 10 firefighters.

Simon-Duplex also was offering the first full-height door in the crew section for models with a raised roof. Slightly awkward looking, this door allowed a firefighter to exit the cab without having to duck his or her head as with other designs. Specific

When Simon-Duplex introduced the D500 Vanguard tilt-cab, it became very popular with Grumman customers. This 1991 unit from West Deptford Township Station 61 in Thorofare, New Jersey, has a 1750-gpm rear-mounted pump. The pump panel, preconnects, and intake ports are located on the side, in place of a storage compartment. The SMFD tilt-cab has characteristic side air vents recessed into the side of the cab.

Beginning with a Duplex D350, the Young Fire Apparatus Company modified the cab with a custom raised roof and full-height bus-style doors for the enclosed crew area. In 1990, the Wayne Township Fire Department ordered six Crusader II pumpers from Young—identical except for the colors. Of the six, Engine 4 was painted bright orange, Engine 1 was white, Engine 2 was yellow, Engine 21 was dark green, Engine 9 was red, and Engine 10 was lime green. The operator panels were located inside the cab enclosure.

model numbers for the Signature Series described the configuration of each particular cab. Examples include a D9400X (extended cab), D9400L (low profile), D9400M (medium profile), and D9400R (raised roof, either 10- or 20-inch). The X, L, M, and R designations could be combined or interchanged, depending on the specific cab in question. The D9500 Signature Series chassis was similar to the D9400 but with fewer options. Only three engine choices were offered and the cab was configured with a medium profile, four doors, and a 7-inch raised roof (MFDR).

The D8400 was available in the Classic and Mark II series. The Classic offered only one cab configuration. This was a flat, four-door model with the shorter "barrier style" doors (MFD). These doors were designed to open fully when the rig is parked next to the cement barrier walls that are on most highways. The full-length doors of the D9400 cabs would require the pumper to remain farther from the wall, which would block traffic and create additional safety hazards for the firefighters. The fully cus-

tom version offering the "barrier style" doors was the Mark II. This offered all of the same customized options and cab configurations as the D9400 Signature Series. Designations were the same as the D9400 models carrying the letters X, M, R, and L after the model number.

Simon decided to divest itself of the companies that it purchased in the U.S. fire apparatus industry in the mid-1990s. Simon also owned LTI (Ladder Towers, Inc.) and was able to find a suitor for this division in 1997. In 1998, Simon was unable to find a buyer for the Duplex chassis division and closed the operation entirely.

Hendrickson

Hendrickson produced custom fire truck chassis for many companies that did not produce their own. The Model 1871—whose model number came from the great Chicago Fire of 1871—could be seen in many departments with bodies by Boardman, Darley, Emergency One, FMC, Grumman, Howe, Pierce, and Pirsch. The unique flat-windshield version with the squared cab was the Model 1871-S (square), which came out in 1973. The 1871-C (contour) was offered with a curved windshield and contour cab in 1976. The standard engine was the six-cylinder, 239-horsepower Detroit Diesel 6-71N.

Hendrickson offered several other engines as options, including the big Detroit 8V-92, eight-cylinder engine, as well as CAT and Cummins models. Optional engines were available up to 475 horsepower. The automatic transmission choices included the Allison MT-643, MT-644, MT-653, and the HT-740D. Manual transmissions from Spicer and Fuller were offered.

When cabs in the industry were widened, Hendrickson introduced the 95-inch-wide 1871-W (wide)beginning in 1980, along with the new 1871-C that was 94-inches wide. The 1871-C and the wider 1871-W provided seating for six firefighters instead of five. The standard for all models had an open jump seat with an option for a fully enclosed four-door model. All cab styles were available in steel or aluminum. The 1871 models were all fixed-cab styles until 1985, when the 1871-WT (wide tilt) was introduced as a tilt-cab version of the squared style. The

first unit with this cab was built as a top-mount pumper for Grumman and was purchased by the fire department in Auke Bay, Alaska, in 1986. In early 1985, the Hendrickson fire truck product line was sold to Kovatch Mobile Equipment (KME), a company that had been supplying various specialty vehicles to the government and military for many years. KME then entered the fire apparatus industry, and later purchased the rights to build the fire truck bodies from Mack, when it left the body building portion of the market.

HME

In late 1985, a new company called HME was formed by purchasers of the remaining assets of the old Hendrickson Mobile Equipment Division. After several years of building specialty Class 8 conventional truck chassis, it designed and produced a series of custom fire truck chassis under private label for Grumman Emergency Products. These chassis, called the Panther series, were produced through 1992. After supplying almost 300 chassis to Grumman, HME began to offer these custom cabs and chassis to all of the apparatus manufacturers in the United States and elsewhere, when Grumman closed the Emergency Products Division in 1992.

A 1980 Towers pumper featuring the popular Hendrickson 84-inch-wide 1871-S cab. This was the premier custom fire truck cab for several years. Towers is a small, Midwest regional apparatus builder. This rig is from Herrin, in southern Illinois, and has a 1500-gpm pump and 750 gallons of water. The interesting side-mount operator's panel has levers and a design that are usually associated with a top-mounted control panel.

In 1986 Auke Bay, Alaska, received the first tilt-cab that was produced by Hendrickson. Fashioned after the 1871-WS cab, the only exterior difference was the front grille. Grumman built the steel Firecat body with a top-mounted console that was exhibited at the New York State Fire Chief's Association trade show that year.

Continuing with the model numbering history of Hendrickson, HME reintroduced the 1871 custom chassis series.

Pemfab

In 1971, Imperial Fire Apparatus entered the fire market, building custom chassis with TCM cabs. In 1975, Imperial was purchased by Pemberton Fabricators and became known as Pemfab. It offered two models. The first was simply the 84 Cab, an 84-inch TCM contoured cab that offered a low-profile version as an option, as well as a fully enclosed four-door version. The rear doors for the four-door model were the same as those used as the front doors. The second model, called the 93 Cab, was also from TCM. This proprietary design for Pemfab was 93 inches wide with a two-piece flat front windshield and a front that sloped in a straight line from the roof to the bumper. The 84 Cab could seat five firefighters, while the 93 Cab could seat six. Both cab styles featured short doors with an exposed step. The standard engine for either model was the Detroit Diesel 6-71N, which was matched with a Spicer five-speed, Fuller T905A, or Allison MT644 transmission.

Pemfab changed the models in the early 1980s to include the 94-inch-wide Maxi series and the new evolution of the 93-inch-wide Wedge. The Maxi was the newest contoured fixed-cab, with an upgraded trim package and full-length doors. This was available as a two-door single-axle (942-S), a two-door tandem-axle (942-T), a four-door single-axle (944-S), and a four-door tandem-axle (944-T) chassis. The Maxi 942 had seating for five, while the Maxi 944 provided seating for seven.

The Wedge was the upgraded 93 Cab. This also had full-length doors now and an upgraded trim package. Models available were the 932-S, 932-T, 934-S, and 934-T, corresponding to the cab width, the number of doors, and the single or tandem rear axles. The 932 had seating for five, and the 934 accommodated seven. The 934 featured a rear door that was notched on an angle for the wheel well, making this a medium four-door (MFD) design. If Pemfab lengthened the cab slightly behind the rear door, that would make this a long medium four-door (LMFD) configuration.

In 1986, the line changed again. The Pemfab Fire Team Line, as it was called, offered five different models with 12 variations, including a new tilt-cab.

The two existing models were carried over into the new line. The Wedge became the Premier. This was available as the S-932 with seating for six and the S-934 with seating for eight. This still was a cab-forward, fixed-cab design. The Maxi became the Royale, which like the Premier, offered additional seating. It was offered as an S-942 stationary six-man canopy cab, and the S-944 eight-man, four-door stationary cab. Instead of depicting the number of axles, the letter designation was moved to the front of the numbering system to indicate a stationary cab (S) or a tilt cab (T).

Pemfab's first model in the tilt-cab market was the Imperial. Beginning with a cab that shared the contoured characteristics of the Premier, the Imperial allowed Pemfab to offer the wide range of cab configurations required to remain competitive in the fire apparatus industry. The Imperial offered a T-942 6-man, full tilt-cab with an

open rear jump seat area. Next in line was the T-942+2. This was a 2-man enclosed cab with no rear seats that tilted, similar to the ER or Stubby cabs produced by other companies for rescue applications. The T-942+4 was a split tilt-cab with seating for 6. This unit had an open jump seat area that remained stationary when the front cab area tilted at the front axle. The next offering was the T-942+8, a 10-man, four-door enclosed split tilt-cab.

Finally, the last Imperial option was the T-944. This was a 10-man, four-door, full tilt-cab model. Both the T-942+8 and the T-944 were long four-door (LFD) models that had straight, full-length rear doors. The Imperial cabs were also available with a raised roof. Pemfab offered raised sections that were 6, 8, 10, or a full 20 inches. Only the 20-inch raised roof was available with windows in the roof extension.

Also in the line now was the Sovereign model. This was a low-profile, stationary-cab design that was available as an SLP-942 with seating for six firefighters. In 1987 it became available as an SLP-944 with seating for eight. The Sovereign was a contoured style that offered a cab 5 inches

This rig was part of the fire brigade at the Lederle Labs plant outside Pearl River, New York. The foam pumper was built by National Foam, and has an elevating platform with a prepiped foam gun. The tandem-axle chassis features the Pemfab Wedge 932-T full-width cab. One characteristic of National Foam units is the lack of a cover over the pump. All of the piping is fully exposed. The pumper was built in 1983 and features a 1,500-gpm pump and a 1,250-gallon foam tank, along with 1,500 pounds of the chemical extinguishing agent, Purple K.

American Eagle was formed in Gainesville, Florida, after several employees left Emergency One to start their own manufacturing company. They built pumpers and aerial bodies, including this unit for the East Sunbury Hose Company Number 1 of Sunbury, Pennsylvania. The chassis is from Pemfab. It is an Imperial T942 full tilt-cab with open jump seats. The "2" signifies a two-door style.

lower than the Royale and 12 inches lower than the Imperial. The final new model was the Marquis. This was a chassis to be customized for body builders with their own unique attributes including special grills and trim packages. It could be built as a forward-control, cab-forward, or cab-over design.

Pemfab cabs were built from aluminum, galvanneal steel, or stainless steel. A full range of engines was offered from 239 to 475 horsepower with transmissions to match each.

When the National Fire Protection Association (NFPA) regulation 1901 was introduced, requiring all fire trucks to have fully enclosed cabs, Pemfab discontinued the open canopy cabs and added SFD and MFD configurations to the line. At the same time, the Premier, Royale, and Sovereign models were discontinued. The entire line was now based on the popular Imperial tilt-cab series.

The new Imperial was distinguishable by a larger front grille, which was 38 inches wide

and 22 inches high. This was recognizable because for the first time it extended below the stainless-steel band that had always wrapped the front of the cab. The design of the grille, however, was not always the same. Pemfab offered custom options for the grille's shape, in addition to cabs that no longer had the decorative stainless-steel band.

The model numbering changed again and became very confusing for all of the configurations that were offered. The line started with the Imperial T962 Series STD (short two-door). This was the ER style for rescue applications without a rear crew area.

The next version was the T964 Series SFD (short four-door). This was the traditional canopy cab that was now enclosed with two rear-facing doors that swung out to a walkway between the cab and body. This was ideally suited for a pumper with a top-mount pump panel. Seating was for four to six firefighters. Other variations of the T964 SFD included the T964 SFDR-20 with a 20-inch raised roof and a T964 SFDR-9 TRE (tall rear entry) with a 9-inch raised roof.

The lineup continued with the Imperial T964 Series MFD (medium four-door). As with all MFD styles, the rear door was notched over the wheel well. This too could be configured with seating for four to six firefighters. There were five configurations available in the MFD series. These were the T964 MFDR-10 (10-inch raised roof), T964 MFDR-10 TRD (tall rear doors), T964 MFDV-20 (20-inch vista roof), and the T964 MFDV-20 TRD. The number after the MFD signified the height of the raised roof. The vista roof had windows in the raised section and the TRD was a full-height side door that extended into the raised roof portion of the cab.

Finally, the Imperial line had the T964 Series LFD (long four-door) models. The rear doors were actually notched MFD doors and not full-length straight doors. The LFD refered to the amount of extended space that existed behind the rear doors. As a comparison, the rear of the MFD cab was 54 inches behind the centerline of the front axle. The LFD cab was either 67.5 inches or available as an optional extended four-door cab (EFD) that went a full 80 inches behind the centerline of the front axle. The LFD cabs had seating for 10 firefighters.

The configurations for these cabs included the T964 LFD, T964 LFDR-10, T964 LFDR-10 TRD, T964 LFDV-20, and the T964 LFDV-20 TRD with all of the designations matching the MFD series.

Pemfab made custom cab designs that were based on the Imperial Series and the Royale Series at one time or another for Boardman, FMC, Gator, and the American LaFrance Pacemaker Series. One of the more unusual modifications was based on the Royale Series. It had a brushed stainless-steel trim package and was meant to

In 1988, Pemfab was supplying the custom Commander chassis for FMC. This can be distinguished by the FMC name stamped into the side grille and the large black plastic band that wraps the front of the cab. This is a Sentinel pumper with a 944 LFD Pemfab full tilt-cab serving Brentwood, Pennsylvania.

Sanford built this pumper in 1987 for the Delaware Engine Company Number 3 in Port Jervis, New York. The top-mount unit has storage racks for firefighters' turn-out gear so they can respond to the scene instead of to the station. The chassis is an early SFD version of the Spartan Gladiator. An aluminum housing with doors has been mounted to the back of the cab. Later versions incorporated the doors as part of the cab.

resemble the discontinued Mack CF cab. After 20 years in the custom fire truck chassis business, Pemfab operations were shut down for good in 1996.

Spartan

Spartan Motors entered into the custom fire truck chassis market in 1975. Spartan also utilized cabs from TCM and changed the way cabs and chassis were sold when it began delivering the units to the original equipment manufacturers (OEMs) fully finished and painted. Up to this time, the cabs were finished with a coat of primer before being delivered to the OEMs. Upon being put into production, each OEM would have to strip the cab's primer and refinish the entire cab, along with the body. Spartan offered a warranty on the entire cab and subsequently decided to ensure the quality of the full cab in an effort to guard against the few OEMs that would not strip the cabs but simply paint over the primer.

Spartan offered the CFV "Maxi-Vision" model in the late 1970s with an 84-inch width. Later, the CFV was available in a 92-inch version. This style combined attributes of a contoured cab with those of a flat cab.

Spartan also offered the CFC custom contour cab that was 84 inches wide. Later, it introduced the 94-inch-wide CFG "Space Master" model with a flat windshield, and the 94-inch CFC "Supercab" that retained its contoured design. The "Supercab" was the predecessor to all of the styles that Spartan currently offers. All models were available in galvanneal steel, stainless steel, or aluminum; offered seating for six firefighters; and were fixed-cab designs. A 2000 or 3000 listing following the three-letter model number denoted the number of axles, two or three, for a particular chassis. The standard engine was the 239-horsepower, six-cylinder, Detroit 6-71N with a Spicer CM60 five-speed transmission. The CFG was a lower-cost alternative to the CFC.

In 1983, the designers at Spartan introduced a new chassis style that was again available with the curved or squared cabs that represented the CFC and CFG styles. Preferring to mount the engine at the front of the chassis to allow for a roomier crew area, but not liking to work under a cab that was tilted overhead, Spartan introduced the Gladiator chassis series. Routine engine maintenance could be performed from inside between the driver's and officer's seats of the cab by way of a hinged cover over the engine that allowed for easy access. For major work or replacement, the engine, transmission, and radiator were mounted on a modular subframe that would roll out after removing the grille enclosure in the face of the cab. The wheelbase started at 140 inches with a 40-degree front tire turn angle.

The Gladiator could accommodate any of the engines available in 1983 up to 445 horsepower. The standard engine was a 250-horsepower Caterpillar Diesel Model 3208T with an Allison MT-644 five-speed automatic transmission. The Gladiator was offered in a standard two-door style in addition to a fully enclosed, four-door, 10-man "Command Cab" version. The Gladiator LFD carried the same designation as the "Space Master" with the addition of a "G" placed at the end. Hence, a two-axle Gladiator would be listed as a CFG-2000G.

The Gladiator was also made available with a new feature that was unique to fire trucks. Fashioning fire truck cabs after those in use for over-the-road trucks, Spartan offered a 20-inch raised roof option. The LFDSC raised roof section was over the rear crew area of the cab and allowed firefighters the room to stand up inside the vehicle. The designers thought this would allow room for a work area for communications equipment, an interior operator's panel for pump controls, or provide space for firefighters to assemble all their personal gear enroute to an emergency. Like American LaFrance's early introduction of the cab-forward design, this "Super Command Cab" was to be a trend that would change fire apparatus design for years to come. Prototype units of the super command cab Gladiator were built for a Grumman pumper, an FMC pumper, and a heavy rescue squad by Frontline.

Spartan adopted a new designation system when it replaced the CFC with the RA20 and RS20 models. The "R" represented the

Darley built this custom Monarch pumper for Oak Park, Illinois. It was the second pumper for Oak Park. This unit has a pump panel enclosed in the LMFDSC cab. Spartan would always accommodate customer requests to alter or upgrade the trim package to match other units or improve the looks of a unit. This is a rear-engine Silent Knight chassis. Upon close examination of the front grille, a solid cab face can be seen. The grille was added to this 1992 pumper to aesthetically match Oak Park's 1988 Darley pumper.

rounded design, the "A" meant aluminum construction, the "S" meant steel, and the "2" stood for the number of axles. The CFG was replaced with the FA20, FS20, and FC20. The "F" signified the flat windshield and the "C" meant stainless-steel construction. Realizing that some customers wanted a tilt-cab, Spartan introduced a version of the Gladiator with a full tilt-cab. At the same time, the flat version was phased out so that all models would have the contoured design. The tilt-cab was available only in the two-door style, while the "Command Cab" and the "Super Command Cab" remained as fixed-cabs with the slide-out engine feature. At the same time, the standard chassis with the engine at the rear of the cab was now known as the Monarch. This cab-forward design was available as a two-door, six-man, or a four-door, eight-man version. The model designation now became MS20, MA20, or MC20, depending on the construction material for the cab. These would not be the last model changes for Spartan.

In 1987, Spartan introduced the Lifesaver chassis. This was to be a state-of-the-art chassis for ambulances and other emergency rescue vehicles. The GVW was 18,000 pounds and the engine options ranged from 190 to 230 horsepower, with an Allison AT545 four-speed or MD-3060 six-speed automatic transmission.

In 1988, Spartan built the first Eurospace cab. This designation was given to a cab interior that was totally open, without a wall between the front and rear passenger compartments. Other manufacturers followed this new and open design in the years to come with models of their own. This first chassis had a pumper body built by Saulsbury and was delivered to the fire department in Lake Saint Louis, Missouri.

In 1989, Spartan adapted all of its cabs to its own new set of standards, called Series 90. The major change was to lower all of the side and door windows to a level that was even with the bottom of the windshield. The window line would be even all the way around the cab from this time forward. The main purpose was to allow the driver to see vehicles and other obstacles closer to the truck. With the lower windows, the driver was now able to see the roof of a compact car outside the passenger front door that was not visible in the spot mirror. This was a big advantage for the driver of any vehicle with a Series 90 cab.

The following year, Spartan mounted the first Detroit Diesel Series 60 engine in a fire truck chassis, and it installed the first Allison World Transmission in a fire truck in 1991.

The Complete Truck Builders
American LaFrance

In 1973, American LaFrance introduced the Century Series chassis, named for the firm's 100 years in business. These units were available in 12-gauge cold-rolled steel as well as stainless steel. They had wider cabs that were replacing the narrower 1000 Series units. Like the preceding designs, the cab was ahead of the engine in the Century Series. Coming at a time when many of the other manufacturers were also bringing out wider cab styles, the Century Series continued the era of the sleek and unique American LaFrance curved design that was very popular. The cab offered seating for a maximum of five people with two rear-facing jump seats under the canopy. The standard engine was the Detroit Diesel 6-71N with an Allison MT-644 automatic transmission, providing a top road speed of 55 miles per hour. The turning radius was 26 feet to either side. Delivery of the Century units began in 1974.

Firefighters rest and check their equipment following a residential house fire. The rig is a 1947 American LaFrance 700 Series open-cab pumper that was retrofitted with a cab roof enclosure. The pump panel is located on the curbside to keep the engineer out of the street.

The Century Series designation referred to a chassis in addition to a complete pumper. American LaFrance was one of the few apparatus builders to also manufacture their own pumps. The Twin-Flow two-stage centrifugal fire pump was the standard pump in American LaFrance products. The company also offered single stage pumps. Capacities available were 1000, 1250, 1500, 1750, and 2000 gallons-per-minute (gpm). The standard water tank on board a Century Series pumper carried 500 gallons. The Century Series was also available in a four-door version, which became a staple within the fleet of the FDNY (Fire Department of New York) between 1980 and 1983 with over 100 units being placed into service.

In the early 1970s, American LaFrance implemented noncosmetic upgrades to the Pioneer Series, which originated in 1964 with a gas engine and a flat angled windshield. This upgraded model, which offered a diesel engine, was known as the Pioneer II. It was the starting-price custom chassis offering from American LaFrance. This model had a large, flat, one-piece windshield and used three wipers. Introduced at the same time as the Century Series, the Pioneer III was released with an upgraded trim package that included stainless-steel trim and black vinyl panels around the turn signals.

In 1976, American LaFrance experimented with a new design that featured a flat windshield tilting in the opposite direction from the Pioneer III. In other words, starting at the base of the windshield, the glass angled backward toward the crew compartment instead of forward and away, as on the Pioneer III. The rear of the cab matched the Century Series design. This design, called the Century Straightline, was not very popular.

An intermediate model by American LaFrance was the Pacemaker Series. This model originated in 1972 and was the step between the Pioneer and the Century. The cab was from TCM and looked similar to many models produced for other manufacturers. The pumper body offered the same features and options as the Century Series as well as the older 900 and 1000 series that were in production prior to this time.

American LaFrance also built pumpers on mass-produced commercial chassis. Under the model names Challenger, Commodore, and Commercial Pumper Series, the same custom body features of a Century pumper were available without the expense of a custom chassis. The Challenger Series was built on medium-duty chassis and offered as standard equipment a 1000-gpm pump, 750-gallon water tank, and six enclosed body compartments. The larger Commodore and Commercial Pumper Series could accommodate any of the Twin-Flow pumps up to 2000 gpm and were most often built on a Ford C-Series chassis. The cab, which came directly from Ford, needed to be modified in most

Between 1980 and 1983, the FDNY purchased over 100 Century pumpers from American LaFrance. Engine 59 had a 1983 1000-gpm pumper with a 500-gallon water tank. FDNY was still ordering pumpers at this time with the hard suction hose mounted over the low-side compartments on the chauffeur's side.

The Haddon Fire Company Number 1 in Haddonfield, New Jersey, has several pumpers from American LaFrance including this 1500-gpm, 1990 Century 2000 Series stainless-steel pumper. The 2000 Series is easily distinguished from the Century Series by the squared headlights and warning lights.

cases with the addition of a rear canopy and bench for three to four firefighters.

The next major product line for American LaFrance came in 1986 with the introduction of the new Century 2000 Series. This was a sleek, updated stainless-steel version of the Century cab that came mated with a 304-L stainless-steel modular body. The cab was available in a two-door, five-man version or a four-door, seven-man configuration. The outward appearance was very modern, with squared headlights, short "barrier style" front doors, and the characteristic American LaFrance flaring of the cab sides over the front axle. American LaFrance produced the cabs and the chassis was initally built by Pemfab. Beginning in October of 1993, HME took over as the chassis supplier for the Century 2000 pumpers, building 27 through 1994. The Century 2000 ceased production in that year.

When the Century 2000 was introduced, American LaFrance continued the Pacemaker Series. Pemfab produced the chassis for American LaFrance. The final American LaFrance style to be introduced, called the Patriot, featured a completely new cab style with slight similarities to the Century models. The chassis was built by HME, and only a few of these units were produced before American LaFrance closed its doors in 1994.

Emergency One

In 1974, a new company emerged from Ocala, Florida, to enter into the expanding industry of fire truck manufacturing. At a time when everyone was using steel to fabricate bodies, Emergency One introduced a complete line of lightweight, nonrusting, aluminum fire trucks. These bodies were also the first in the fire service to feature modular construction. Other companies formed their bodies on the chassis from start to finish. The Emergency One bodies were built separately from the chassis and then mounted upon their completion. Emergency One also boasted a 30- to 60-day delivery time, the fastest in the fire industry.

The large Emergency One product line began with the Series 10060 minipumpers. These were available on two-wheel drive and four-wheel drive 11,000-pound GVW commercial pickup truck chassis. They featured 260 gallons of water, a 250-gpm Hale power take-off (PTO) pump and 200 feet of 1-inch booster line on a reel that was centered above the pump panel.

The next models included the 15060 and 20084 Quick Attack Rescue Pumpers (midipumpers). These were available on two-wheel drive and four-wheel drive medium-duty commercial chassis and featured the same 250-gpm Hale PTO pump. The 15060 came with a 300-gallon water tank on a 14,000-pound GVW chassis, while the 20084 had a 500-gallon tank and a 25,000-pound GVW chassis. Both models also had a booster reel. Externally, the difference was obvious in the longer body

of the 20084, which had a vertical compartment between the pump panel and the rear axle. Two variations of the 20084 were offered later, including the 20084M, which had a 500- or 750-gpm pump, and the 20084TC with the 250-gpm PTO pump and a Ford C-Series tilt-cab chassis.

The 20102 midipumper followed. This series offered a Class A pumper to fill the void between low-volume attack pumpers and full-size Class A pumpers. Again, these were offered on two-wheel drive and four-wheel drive medium-duty commercial chassis, with a GVW of 25,000 pounds and a 500-gallon booster tank. The new feature separating these from the 20084 series was a 500- or 750-gpm Hale midship-mounted pump. Standard features included a booster reel, double crosslay hose beds for 1 1/2-inch attackline, and a larger rear hose bed to achieve a full rating for the unit.

Moving up the product line, the next entry was the Guardsman Series, which also used a 25,000-pound GVW , medium-duty chassis. Here, the options included a choice of a 500, 750, or 1,000-gallon water tank in addition to a Hale midship pump ranging from 500- to 1000- gpm. Additional choices for the body design became available with this series, which was Emergency One's most economical, commercial Class A pumper.

Emergency One also had the Sentry Series commercial pumper. The Sentry I was the smallest Class A pumper to incorporate all of the features required by NFPA 1901. Built on a 149-inch wheelbase, 25,000-pound GVW medium-duty chassis, the Sentry I had a 500-gallon water tank and a Hale 1000-gpm pump. Standard features included liquid-filled gauges and a booster reel above the pump panel. The Sentry III was built on a Ford C-Series chassis that was most often modified with a rear canopy and

A 1976 American LaFrance Pioneer II pumper sits in the rain after a house fire in suburban Illinois. This model can be distinguished from the Pioneer III by the simple trim package and plain front. Later models also were produced with a third windshield wiper.

Winter Park, Florida, purchased this ALS-equipped commercial E-One pumper in 1982. Built on a Ford F700 Series chassis, the custom enclosure behind the cab has a gurney for patient transport. Years ahead of its time, this pumper consolidated two units into one. This was also a full Class-A pumper with a 1000-gpm pump and 500-gallon water tank.

bench for additional crew seating. The choice of pumps ranged from 500- to 1000-gpm and the standard 500-gallon booster tank could be upgraded to hold 750 or 1,000 gallons. This was the first model available with a top-mounted operator's control panel, giving the pump operator 360-degree visibility of the fire scene. Emergency One was proud that the lightweight aluminum body could save as much as 4,000 pounds of truck weight, allowing a fire department to carry more water or equipment, while saving wear and tear on the brakes and chassis.

The top-of-the-line unit was in the Protector Series. These units were available with side- or top-mounted pump controls. The Protector I featured a GMC 6500, 25,000-pound GVW, medium-duty commercial chassis in either two- or four-wheel drive. Water tanks of 500- or 750-gallon capacities were offered, as well as pumps ranging from 500 to 1000 gpm. When ordered with a side pump panel, the Protector I units had a front

transverse compartment between the cab and pump panel, in addition to twin crosslay hose beds above this compartment.

The Protector II series featured the Ford C-Series tilt-cab chassis, as supplied from the factory, with no additional seating. The Protector III added the canopy extension to the Ford tilt-cab, providing seating for five. Both models incorporated all of the same features and options as the Protector I.

The Protector IV models were the first to offer fire departments the choice of a custom chassis from one of several manufacturers—Hendrickson, Spartan, Duplex, or Pemfab. The available pump options ranged from 1000 to 2000 gpm, and the water tanks ranged from the standard of 500 gallons to an optional 750- or 1,000-gallon capacity. One booster reel was still standard, along with the transverse compartment and crosslay hose beds. Emergency One also fabricated an aluminum, diamond plate enclosure over the engine.

Emergency One offered its line of custom fire trucks on chassis that were built specially for the fire service by others. When other manufacturers were going into the custom chassis business as an extension of bodybuilding, Emergency One was preparing to do the same.

Emergency One's first custom chassis model came in 1984 with the introduction of the cab-forward Hurricane. The Hurricane cab was initially available in a squared version with a flat windshield and three wipers. Built completely of 1/4-inch aluminum, as compared to 1/8-inch for the competitors, this custom chassis became very popular. The Hurricane was released as a two-door model with open, rear-facing jump seats, or with the option for a fully enclosed four-door (LFD) version. It also offered the largest side window in the industry for the firefighters in the rear jump seats. The standard engines were from Detroit Diesel with Cummins engines offered as an option. The Hurricane was available for pumpers, rescues, and aerials and could be ordered with either two-, four-, or six-wheel drive.

When the Hurricane was introduced, Emergency One expanded the Sentry Series to include a Sentry IV that would incorporate a custom chassis. The Hurricane could then be ordered with a Sentry IV or Protector IV series body style.

The Sentry IV and Protector IV Series were expanded to include water tanks with capacities of up to 1,500 gallons, with the same pump options. Production time was still the shortest in the fire industry, although it now stretched from 30 to 90 days.

Emergency One was offering a total of 24 different models of commercial pumpers, ranging from the minipumper to the Protector III with the canopy cab.

Pumper styles were grouped into three categories, light response vehicles, commercial pumpers, and custom pumpers. The light response vehicles started with the 10060 minipumper that now carried 200 gallons of water and a choice of 250- or 350-gpm PTO pumps. The 15060 and 20084 midipumpers, as well as the 20084TC, carried the same amounts of water as before but now had the option of the 350-gpm PTO

pumps. There was no change in the 20084M or the 20102 series pumpers.

The commercial pumpers consisted of the Protector I, Protector I TM, Protector II, Protector III, Guardsman, Sentry I, Sentry III, and the Sentry III TM. The Guardsman and Sentry models remained the same with the exception of a 750-gallon booster tank that was now available for the Sentry I. The only change in the Protector Series was the availability of water tanks with up to 1,000-gallon capacities.

The Protector IV and Sentry IV Series were now being shown with the Hurricane chassis, but they were still available with the customer's choice of other custom chassis. Here too the maximum capacity water tank was increased, to allow up to 1,500 gallons. Later in the year, the Hurricane was also offered with a contoured design in addition to the original version with the flat windshield and cab face.

In 1985, Federal Motors began operations. Located in one of the buildings at the Emergency One plant, this new company took over the building of chassis, while Emergency One built bodies and aerial devices. Federal Motors produced the Hurricane custom fire truck cab and chassis in addition to specialized chassis that were sold to other industrial markets. These included such products as off-road drill rigs and a trackless trolley bus for public transportation companies.

The chassis options were expanded in 1985 with the introduction of the Hush model at the International Association of

Ward LaFrance utilized this four-piece angled windshield design as the trademark look for its Ambassador Series cab. This 1969 pumper has an elevating command tower located above the pump enclosure. Note the hard suction hose mounted above the low-side compartments on the driver's side.

Fire Chiefs Convention in New Orleans. The Hush offered a wide-open cab with no interior motor compartment, commonly referred to as a doghouse. This was due to the fact that the engine was mounted at the rear of the chassis' frame rails instead of at the very front or midship. The Hush promised both the roomiest and the quietest cab on the market. The obstruction between the front and rear seats could be removed, allowing additional options for the cab design. The Hush offered seating for up to nine firefighters in a flat-roof, LFD cab. The personnel would no longer have to compete with the noises from the motor while trying to communicate with each other, prompting the Hush name.

The Hush was available in both SMFD and LFD cab configurations. The SMFD version featured an optional storage compartment between the driver's door and the rear door, while the LFD had an extra-wide window there.

The Hush offered many product enhancements. It was the first pumper design that eliminated the rear step at the back of the body. Other options included warning devices to indicate open compartments and back-up alarms to reduce the risk of firefighter injuries. The Hush also featured special red lights inside the cab to minimize the effect on a firefighter's eyes when exiting the cab at night. Another new idea put the air horns and siren in the front bumper to reduce cab noise generated from the traditional cab roof placement.

This was really the first major design change since the release of the super command cab by Spartan. Although it seemed to revolutionize custom fire truck chassis, the Hush was a costly, high-end option for fire departments.

A year later came the release of the Cyclone chassis. This was another cab-forward, fixed-cab design that offered more headroom than the Hurricane. The basic cab shell was the same, with the modifications needed for the increased height. This featured a contoured cab design with a two-piece curved windshield similar in

The Chicago Fire Department purchased E-One apparatus for many years. This is an example of an early E-One Hurricane cab with the flat front. Chicago specified the extended front bumper to carry LDH for a supply line.

appearance to the contoured version of the Hurricane. The Cyclone, though, had smaller windows than the Hurricane on the front doors and at the rear jump seat positions. The Cyclone windows were level with the bottom of the windshield line, while the Hurricane windows extended to a point lower than the front windshield.

By 1987, the Hush had become the Hush XL. It was now offered in a full variety of cab configurations that would accommodate up to 12 firefighters. Some of the options included SMFD, SMFDSC, LFD, and LFDSC with interior mobile command posts, interior pump controls, and different seating layouts. Body styles for pumpers allowed both side and top-mounted operator's controls, and there were also aerials and rescue squad applications that used the Hush Series. Like all Emergency One chassis, the Hush could be ordered as a two-wheel drive or four-wheel drive model. A multitude of engines were available from Detroit Diesel, Cummins, and Caterpillar, fitted with automatic transmissions from Allison. Water tanks from 500 to 1,000 gallons and pumps from 1000 to 2000 gpm were also available. Due to their unique design,

Hush XL pumpers were a new custom designation in the product line-up that did not correspond to the Protector or Sentry Series.

The Protector IV Series was replaced with the Protector XL Series and was offered on the Cyclone and Hurricane chassis. Both cabs were still available with open, rear-facing jump seats. Fully enclosed four-door versions were optional for both models. The Protector XL pumpers were available with water tanks from 500 to 1,000 gallons and 1000 to 2000-gpm pumps. The top-mounted model was called the Protector XLT.

That same year, the pumper product line was simplified. Now there were custom pumpers, commercial pumpers, and quick attack pumpers. The model number designations were reduced, simplifying the process of comparing what each variation offered.

Custom pumpers were built on a Cyclone, Hurricane, or Hush XL chassis. The first two used a Protector XL or XLT body style that offered a combination of options. The Hush XL offered its own unique body style that was tailored to the rear engine design and could also be customized.

Commercial pumpers were built on conventional or tilt-cab chassis from Ford,

For many years, the Crown Firecoach Company built the bulk of all apparatus on the West Coast. The Los Angeles City and County fire departments purchased Crown almost exclusively. Most of the rigs had open-cab roofs, such as this 1967 1500-gpm Engine 89, owned by the city of Los Angeles.

A 1982 Mack 1250-gpm pumper on the MC Series chassis with a full-width rear-facing bench seat for the firefighters. The characteristic Mack body includes beavertail compartments beneath a diamond-plate panel with curved edges.

GMC, Chevrolet, International, or Mack and could be modified with a canopy for additional seating. The most common engines were the Caterpillar 3208T or the Detroit 8.2T with automatic or manual transmissions. Depending on the style, a fire department could get a water tank with a capacity ranging from 500 to 1,000 gallons and pump outputs from 750 to 1250 gpm. Side- or top-mounted pump controls were available as well as customization of the body style and compartments.

Quick attack pumpers also used commercial chassis that were either conventional or tilt-cab styles. The 10060 minipumper, as well as the 15060 midipumper, remained unchanged. The 20084 midipumper now offered a 750-gpm PTO driven pump as an option, whereas the 20102 midipumper now offered midship pumps up to 750 gpm.

By 1988, Emergency One had unofficially become E-One.

In 1989, the Cyclone was offered with the longer jump seat windows like the Hurricane. In addition, the LFD version used the same doors as the LFD Hurricane. Both models could seat up to eight firefighters. From the outside, the Cyclone had a different trim package than the Hurricane. The Hush XL pumpers were now offered with water

tanks not to exceed 1,250 gallons. The commercial pumpers also used the Protector XL and XLT body designations. There were no changes to the Quick Attack Pumpers.

In 1990, the quick attack pumpers became quick attack vehicles and were either minipumpers or midipumpers. The minipumpers were offered with 250- to 450-gpm pumps and 150- to 300-gallon water tanks. The midipumpers had a choice of 250- to 750-gpm pumps with water tanks from 300 to 500 gallons.

The full-size pumper line was changed to include nine models. Individual body styles and classes were gone and the chassis type dictated the model for the pumper, since all bodies could be custom designed. These models included the conventional commercial pumper, Town & Country pumper, tilt-cab commercial pumper, Protector Pumper, Cyclone Pumper, Hurricane Pumper, Hush Pumper, Hush Vista Pumper, and the Cyclone TC Pumper.

The conventional commercial pumper and the tilt-cab commercial pumper offered 750- to 1250-gpm pumps with 500- to 1,000-gallon water tanks. The Town & Country featured an International 4000 Series chassis with either a two- or four-door cab with the same tank and pump options as the other commercial models.

The Protector, a fixed-cab model, was introduced as E-One's first chassis featuring an engine-forward design. This was a lower-cost model that only offered a 6CTA 8.3 Cummins engine. Cab configurations were initially limited to an MFD and were later expanded to include an SMFD and LFD. This fixed-cab then became E-One's first tilt-cab style. The chassis was available only with two-wheel drive. This model would accommodate 1000- to 1500-gpm pumps and 500 to 1,000 gallons of water, and engines with 250 to 300 horsepower. A large, square grille was in the middle of the cab face that had eight vertical columns of small cutouts. There was also a small grille on the side of the cab that was notched and rested at the top of the wheel well in the fender. The Protector had a GVW range from 35,000 to 38,000 pounds. Along with the introduction of the tilt-cab, options for seating, trim packages, and engines were expanded.

The Cyclone still offered two-wheel drive or four-wheel drive models. It was available with 1000- to 2000-gpm pumps and tanks to hold from 500 to 1,000 gallons. The Hurricane had all of the same options as the Cyclone. Another addition to the chassis line-up now was the Cyclone TC, which was another tilt-cab. This was available with 750- to 2000-gpm pumps and water tanks to hold from 500 to 1,000 gallons. The cab face had the same large grille as the Protector, as well as the side grilles. This unit had a larger doghouse and accommodated larger engines than the Protector. It had a GVW range that started where the Protector left off, at 38,000 pounds, and went to 51,000 pounds. This now superseded all of the other chassis available from E-One.

The Protector TC and the Cyclone TC were virtually indistinguishable from the outside, although the Protector TC used automotive windshield wipers, while the Cyclone TC used parallelogram wipers. Inside, they had different dashboards.

The Hush pumper again could be ordered with tanks holding up to 1,000 gallons and 750- to 2000-gpm pumps. The Hush Vista pumper had a 19-inch raised roof with windows all the way around. The side door was an SMFD style but the cab roof extended beyond the side door going over the pump. This model had an interior top-mounted operator's panel in addition to all of the available features of the regular Hush pumper.

Mack

Mack's first custom cab-forward design was the C-Series, with the C-85 and C-95 introduced in 1957. This was replaced in 1967 by the wider CF Series, one of the most popular custom fire truck chassis ever built. Mack built custom pumpers on the CF chassis for fire departments up and down the East Coast, as well as cities as far away as California. Featuring Mack's own Maxidyne diesel engines and power trains, the distinctive CF was always one of the quietest pumpers on the fireground. It was available with 235- through 350-horsepower engines. The FDNY was by far the largest customer for the CF pumpers. It began to buy them in 1968 with conventional two-door canopy

FDNY Engine 277 was one of six pumpers that were part of an experiment in 1981 to test the visibility of lime green versus red for the safety of responding fire trucks. Eventually, all rigs were returned to the traditional red. This is a four-door CF with a 1000-gpm pump. FDNY covered the hose beds with tarps for many years to keep the hose clean and free of debris that might be thrown from buildings.

cabs. In 1971, the pumpers arrived with fully enclosed four-door crew cabs. Nearly 400 Mack CF pumpers were delivered to New York by 1983, when Mack ceased production of fire apparatus.

As an independent chassis builder, Mack offered the CF chassis to other companies that would build the bodies. Ward '79 began to build the FDNY pumpers using the Mack CF chassis and, delivered over 100 of these units between 1984 and 1989, when Ward '79 closed its doors. The CF chassis was discontinued in 1990.

Mack also offered the MC cab-over split tilt-cab chassis and the R Series conventional chassis. These chassis were also produced for markets other than the fire service. The MS Series was another Mack chassis. This was from a design by Renault, which bought into Mack in the early 1980s. The MC series engines featured 210 through 283 horsepower,

the R Series offered 248 through 350 horsepower, and the MS utilized smaller 175- through 210-horsepower engines.

Pierce

In the early 1970s, Pierce offered a complete line of fire apparatus that included 10 distinct products. In pumpers, it had the initial attack pumper, plus the Minuteman, Suburban 750, Suburban 1000, HD Suburban, tanker, and the Fire Marshal pumper. Pierce also had aerials and two types of rescue apparatus.

The initial attack pumper used a small 3/4-ton two-wheel drive or four-wheel drive Chevrolet K-30, Ford F-350, or Dodge W-400 chassis. These minipumpers were made of aluminum and offered a 250- or 400-gpm PTO driven pump. They were equipped with 250-gallon water tanks and one electric rewind booster reel that carried 200 feet of 1-inch rubber hose.

The Minuteman was a midipumper that was slightly larger than the minipumper. It was able to carry more hose, equipment, water, and a larger pump, with capacities ranging from 250 to 1000 gpm. Like the minipumper, the Minuteman had an aluminum body. Based on the pump configuration, there were six variations in the Minuteman Series that were designated I, II, III, IV, V, and VI. The I and II were based on PTO-driven pumps. The III through VI offered midship pumps. In the early 1980s, the Minuteman Series were built on a medium-duty commercial chassis. In the late 1980s, when Pierce introduced its own custom chassis, the Minuteman Series could be purchased with any of the custom chassis in addition to the commercial chassis.

The next model in the line was the Suburban 750. Similar to the Minuteman, this model used a medium-duty, conventional commercial cab and chassis, but offered a custom-built Pierce body. A 750 or 1000-gpm pump was offered with 500-, 750- or 1,000-gallon water tanks. This series was meant to offer a lower-cost alternative to the larger models by utilizing a smaller and more economical chassis. The standard body was fabricated from galvanneal steel, although aluminum was an option. Though most bodies featured high-side compartments on the driver's side, it was not uncommon to find a less-expensive design that used the space for hard suction hose instead of additional compartments. In the late 1980s, the pump and tank options were increased.

The Suburban 1000 series was the most popular model until the full introduction of the custom chassis. Even then its popularity continued for many years for departments that did not want the added expense of a custom chassis. This unit featured a commercial tilt-cab chassis to reduce the overall length, improve the turning radius, and increase the driver's visibility as compared with a conventional chassis.

For all practical purposes, the only chassis used for the Suburban 1000 was the Ford C-Series. Most often, the customer had Pierce fabricate a rear canopy and jump seat

This cream-colored 1986 Pierce Arrow pumper is from the Elkins Park Volunteer Fire Company, Cheltenham Township, Pennsylvania. It features an early cab design with open, rear-facing jump seats for the crew.

In 1986, the volunteer fire department in Clinton, Maryland, purchased the most expensive pumper that had been built to date by Pierce. It featured an LFD Lance cab and chassis with the original grille design. The engine was equipped with a 2000-gpm capacity pump, a vertical chrome exhaust pipe on the curbside, and a 500-gallon water tank. It had more emergency lights than many departments had on two pumpers.

for firefighter seating. Basically, two body styles were offered. These differed by having two or three upper compartments on the driver's side of the body. Pump and tank options were the same as the 750 series.

The HD Suburban used larger chassis than the 1000 series, along with bigger engines and optional larger pumps. These were marketed as an equally powerful alternative to custom chassis with the serviceability and price tag of a commercial chassis. A modified cab was also pretty much standard for most departments.

Pierce offered a line of custom pumpers that were built on the Hendrickson 1871-S chassis. Called the Fire Marshal series, these pumpers wre available with pumps up to 1500 gpm and 500 to 1,000 gallon water tanks. Chassis from other companies could also be ordered, but Hendrickson was the primary supplier.

The Pierce Arrow cab style took the market by storm when Pierce introduced it

in 1979. It offered a wide 94-inch design with a contoured front and curved windshield. Similar to the TCM cabs, the front area had a driver's seat plus bench seating for two additional firefighters. The design allowed the entire front cab interior area to be clear from side to side. The rear-facing jump seats were on either side of the motor. The cab could accommodate up to four firefighters in addition to the driver. Built on a chassis that was originally constructed by Oshkosh, the Pierce Arrow designation referred to both the body and the cab. It became extremely popular.

After just a few short years, Pierce began total production of the chassis and cab in its own plants in 1982. In the years to come, the name was to be used solely for the chassis reference when it was also made available for aerials, tankers, and rescue squads. Pierce made bodies of galvanneal steel or aluminum and offered only Waterous pumps.

The Arrow cab had an optional fully enclosed four-door (LFD) version. The standard engine was the 330-horsepower Detroit Diesel 6V-92TA, along with a four-speed Allison HT-740 automatic transmission. In an effort to help the pump operator, Pierce covered its pump panels with black vinyl to minimize the glare on a sunny day. This became a Pierce trademark.

The success of the Pierce Arrow chassis design was followed by the introduction of the Dash series chassis. The prototype unit was built in 1981, although production did not start until 1983. The Dash was the first custom tilt-cab introduced by Pierce and was fabricated from aluminum. This was a full tilt-cab design with a wheelbase that was initially 30 inches shorter than the Arrow. The design of the Dash interior, and

the corresponding seating capacities, depended on the customer's choice of engine.

The standard engine was the Detroit Diesel 8.2T, which allowed a driver's seat and full bench in the front. For models with all engines except the standard, the motor was moved forward and sat between the driver and officer. The jump seat area provided two seats that were on either side of the doghouse in both styles. This meant that the Dash would accommodate five firefighters with the standard engine or four firefighters with any other engine choice. Beginning in 1986, the standard engine was the 350-horsepower Detroit Diesel 6V-92TA, which meant the cab was configured to seat only four persons. The standard transmission at the time was the four-speed automatic Allison HT-740. Water tanks from 500 to 1,500 gallons were available,

Palm Beach Gardens, Florida, purchased two Javelin pumpers from Pierce in 1990. These were outfitted with 1250-gpm pumps, 750-gallon water tanks, and 50-gallon foam tanks around the pump. The engine was mounted over the rear axle and the large shape between the cab and pump panel was the water tank.

along with a side or top-mounted pump panel. Starting in 1989, the Dash was solely a four-person cab.

Pierce introduced another version of the Dash in 1984. Known as the Dash D-8000, this version offered only the 250-horsepower Caterpillar 3208T-turbocharged engine with the Allison MT-643 transmission. This model was introduced to combat the popularity of the Ford C-8000 series. Both had the same engine, though the D-8000 offered a custom fire truck cab without the expenses associated with most of them. The cab was similar to the conventional Dash with the exception of the location of the front grille. The D-8000 had a low grille that extended upward from behind the front bumper without touching the decorative steel band. The standard Dash had a similar grille located within the stainless-steel trim band, between the headlights. Pierce marketed the D-8000 as a complete unit, as opposed to a pumper modified around a commercial chassis.

Pierce continued to expand its line of custom chassis with the introduction of the Lance series in 1985. The Lance was a split tilt-cab. The engine was again located up front, so only the forward portion of the cab, the front seat area, tilted for engine access and maintenance. Unlike the Dash, the Lance offered a full bench seat under the

canopy that accommodated four firefighters. This made the Lance a six-person cab with the capability to seat even more. Once the Lance was in production, cab configurations increased significantly. Like the Dash, the Lance had a short wheelbase of 163 inches. The engine was installed between the frame rails instead of resting on them, thanks to an offset design at the front. This lowered the center of gravity to provide superior stability and handling over models with straight rail chassis frames.

The growing popularity of fully enclosed cabs gave a Lance purchaser the option of a simple four-door enclosure (LFD) or an extended four-door enclosure (XLFD) with room to seat up to 10 persons. In addition, there was now a 20-inch raised-roof version of both enclosures (LFDSC and XLFDSC) that allowed firefighters to stand up in the crew section. Designs for the extended and raised crew compartments included mobile command posts, an interior top-mounted operator's panel, seating for 8, or space for a stretcher allowing patient transport to the hospital.

The Lance used the same standard engine as the Arrow and was initially offered with a Pierce Arrow body. In 1987, to eliminate confusion, the body was designated a Pierce Lance body. The Lance was introduced with a large grille in the front of the cab for cooling the engine. Its original design had a vertical and horizontal pattern that was flush with the face of the cab. In 1987, the grille pattern changed to a louvered design with only horizontal members. It had a heavier frame surrounding it and protruded from the face of the cab.

By the early 1990s, Ford had discontinued the C-8000 series tilt-cab, and the majority of commercial chassis for fire trucks became the IHC 4900 Series and the Freightliner Business Class Series. Without the tilt-cab, the distinction between the Suburban 750 and Suburban 1000 series was lost. Now it was known simply as the Suburban Series and represented custom bodies built on commercial chassis. By this time, it was also mandated that all new fire apparatus provide space for firefighters to be within an enclosed cab while the vehicle is in motion. Both IHC and Freightliner offered four-door crew cabs allowing the Suburban program to meet this requirement. The Suburban Series was offered in galvanneal steel with a choice of water tanks holding 500, 750, or 1,000 gallons.

Pierce introduced another pumper style in 1990 called the Javelin, a new design that incorporated the cab, chassis, and body together. The Javelin was a front-wheel drive fire truck that offered an antilock braking system (ABS) as well as electronic traction control. The exterior cab shell was that of the Pierce Arrow with an MFD configuration. The engine was mounted behind the fire pump over the rear axle, giving a spacious and open cab interior with seating options for up to 11 firefighters. Eight could fit in the crew area of an extended cab (LMFD) with a driver, officer, and additional firefighter in the front.

The Javelin also introduced a new shape and location for the water tank. Steel tanks with capacities of 500, 750, or 1,000 gallons were placed between the cab and the pump, offering an added buffer to reduce noise in the cab.

The Detroit Diesel 6V92-TA 350-horsepower was the standard engine along with the Allison HT-741 four-speed automatic transmission. A side-mounted operator's panel was the only available

configuration with the Javelin. To allow for cooling the engine, a grille was built into the diamond plate under the hose bed along the rear of the unit.

In 1991, Pierce offered a 22-inch raised-roof option for the Javelin Series. The cab configurations available at that time included the MFD, MFDSC, LMFD, and the LMFDSC. Since the water tank was visible and placed between the cab and pump, the overall vehicle length would vary by the capacity. A 500-gallon tank was half the width of a 1,000-gallon tank, which made the capacity readily apparent by looking at the unit.

Seagrave

Seagrave introduced its modern cab-forward design in 1959. The 86-inch-wide P-Series offered a clean-looking cab with a two-piece curved windshield that would find a home in many fire stations throughout the United States. The P-Series was upgraded in 1972 to the diesel-powered PB-Series. Unlike other manufacturers that offered TCM cabs, Seagrave has always fabricated its own custom cabs.

Seagrave produced another chassis series during the lifetime of the PB-Series. Designated the SR-Series, this was a low-profile version of the same cab that was produced for aerials. The "S" represented the lower cab design and the "R" designated a rear-mount aerial with a two-wheel drive chassis.

The Patton Bridgeton Terrace Fire Protection District near St. Louis, Missouri, purchased this Seagrave pumper, featuring the low-profile WB Series cab and chassis, in 1978. This full-width cab has the black rubber "zip" gaskets around the front access panels that were introduced with the H and W Series.

The engineer helps a firefighter grab a preconnected attack line off a 1972 Seagrave PB-Model custom pumper. The exposed fenders indicate the 84-inch-wide P-Series.

In 1978, Seagrave introduced the W-Cab. The W-Cab was a low-profile 92-inch-wide cab for pumpers and aerials. The W-Cab featured a full-length front door due to the height change. Pumper chassis were designated WB.

In 1979, Seagrave brought out a new custom cab that was 94 inches wide. This new H-Series cab kept the same lines of the P-Series with a broader front and minimal fenders. The driver's step was exposed and Seagrave installed a small grille on each side of the cab behind the door to allow heat to escape from the larger engines. With the W-Cab, Seagrave initiated the use of access panels on the face of the cab for servicing wiring and other components. These characteristic panels were outlined with black rubber "zip" gaskets. The rubber permitted relatively easy removal and replacement of these panels, and provided the very distinctive look of Seagrave cabs from that point forward. Pumpers were labeled HB for standard drive and HD if they had four-wheel drive. The H-Cab was produced in small quantities with a fully enclosed four-door cab. These early cabs used the same doors for the rear crew enclosure as were used for the front doors.

Seagrave made a military-style pumper available for the civilian market in 1983. Called the Invader Series, this was a less-expensive, no-frills, square-cab design that carried the MB designation. The Invader cab was very plain and did not prove to be very popular, and production ceased after a few short years.

Sutphen

The Sutphen Company started building custom pumpers in the early 1970s. It offered fire departments a choice of mass-produced commercial chassis or Sutphen's own custom chassis. In the early years, the majority of these units were sold to departments in Ohio, the company's home state. The custom chassis used a TCM cab trimmed out in a very distinctive manner that made a Sutphen pumper easy to spot. Sutphen dressed the cab front with two or three stainless-steel moldings between the windshield, the warning lights, and the headlights. Sutphen also used two large stainless-steel housings on each side of the cab's face. The upper housing held three round warning lights. These were the turn signals and hazard flashers, as well as part of the complement of alternating "en-route" lights that combined with the rotating beacons and strobes to alert others of an emergency response. The lower and larger housing contained the headlights and high beams.

As early as 1974, Sutphen was also offering a four-door model to fire departments that requested it. Initially, Sutphen utilized the industry-standard 84-inch contoured cab and then upgraded to the 94-inch model when it was released.

By the late 1970s, Sutphen had acquired a substantial following throughout the Midwest and expanded along the eastern seaboard as far south as Florida. Known mainly for its unique aerial platforms, Sutphen pumpers were added by many departments that had accepted one or more of the aerials.

Body Builders
Darley

Throughout the 1960s and 1970s, the W. S. Darley Company featured economical pumpers on commercial chassis. It built minipumpers, full-sized pumpers, and pumper-tankers. The Challenger Series featured a conventional commercial chassis from Ford, International, GMC, or Dodge. It offered a variety of body styles with low-side, high-side, or no side compartments. Although the pump panel was most often on the side, Darley also built a front-mounted series and a top-mounted version. Water tanks from 250 to 1,200 gallons and Darley's own brand of Champion fire pumps up to 1750 gpm were available. A 750-gpm model was standard.

If it had a midship pump, it was a Challenger S750, while the same unit with a front-mounted pump was an RF750. The front-mounted pump allowed for a larger water tank, easy drafting, in addition to pump and roll capabilities.

The Monarch Series was next, and featured a Ford, Chevrolet, or Dodge tilt-cab chassis. Pumps were available up to 1250 gpm and the standard 750-gallon water tank could also be increased. Both models,

the Challenger and the Monarch, were available as stock units but could be ordered with a minimal range of customized options to allow each department to tailor the apparatus to its needs.

In 1973 when Hendrickson introduced the 1871 custom chassis, Darley offered a line of custom pumpers using this chassis as a step up from the Monarch Series. The custom-designed bodies were similar, but the new cab options became popular.

In 1989, Darley introduced the Engager Series, which was designed to meet the proposed NFPA 1901 specifications. It featured Darley's own 1250-gpm Champion pump, a top-mounted control panel, fully extended compartmentation, and a fully enclosed Spartan tilt-cab that was available with seating for up to eight people.

At this time, the Darley line included four pumper models, available in galvanneal

The Invader pumper series that Seagrave introduced in 1983 did not prove to be very popular. Based on a design that Seagrave offered to the military, the MB Series was a no-frills, low-cost, plain pumper. This 1983 1250-gpm pumper went to St. Charles, Illinois.

steel or aluminum. The bodies were "all-custom" applications with the various models using different types of chassis.

The Challenger Series still featured a conventional commercial chassis. The available pumps ranged from 750 to 1500 gpm with water tanks from 500 to 1,500 gallons. Darley offered custom cab enclosures as well as four-door conversions for additional seating.

The Monarch Series followed the specs of the Challenger Series but used a commercial tilt-cab chassis. Again, Darley would provide fully enclosed seating arrangements to accommodate up to six people.

Next came the Engager Series with custom SFD or MFD tilt-cabs and up to 300-horsepower engines. The top-of-the-line series was the Patriot, which offered a full line of custom chassis, including the larger Super Command Cabs with bigger engines. Darley also specialized in unique pump panel designs, which were placed on the top, side, front, rear, or enclosed inside the cab.

FMC

The Fire Apparatus Division of FMC was based in Tipton, Indiana, between 1970 and 1986. It was known largely for its economical pumpers, built on mass-produced commercial chassis without an abundance of trim and upgrade options. It was not uncommon to find an FMC pumper in the majority of volunteer rural departments throughout the United States on a Ford or Chevy chassis.

In the 1970s, FMC had two main lines of fire trucks. The first was simply called the FMC Commercial Firefighters. These pumpers were built on any of the available commercial chassis from Ford or Chevrolet. FMC offered its own twin-stage fire pump in addition to the option of a Hale brand single- or twin-stage pump. Pump capacities ranged from 500 to 1750 gpm with water tanks up to 2,500 gallons. Units were available with midship or front-mounted pumps. The booster reels were mounted just behind the cab on top of the midship pump and were usually enclosed in a metal-covered housing that opened for access when needed. Emblazoned with the FMC or Bean logo, this characteristic design distinguished these pumpers from the competition.

The Commercial Firefighter also offered the FMC Semi-Custom. This unit started with a Ford C-Series chassis that had a Detroit Diesel engine and an Allison transmission. Pumps up to 1500 gpm and an optional modified canopy cab were intended to provide all the benefits of a custom pumper without sacrificing the economy and service of a commercial chassis.

The Commercial line also had the FMC HPV and the FMC QAV. The HPV was a Class A pumper that combined a Class A volume pump with an FMC high-pressure fog pump. These units also featured pump and roll capabilities due to the PTO drive on the high-pressure pump. The QAV pumper was a quick-attack vehicle with a short-body design for improved maneuverability and a short turning radius. This model introduced the noncurved, angular rear wheel well cutouts that would be carried into future lines as classic FMC styling. The other models had curved wheel wells.

FMC also had the Custom Firefighters. These were built around custom chassis from Spartan Motors. Two 84-inch-wide cab and chassis options were available, the CFS-2000 and the CFV-2000. The CFS-2000, Spartan's Supercab Series, had a curved windshield, contoured TCM-style cab with windshield glass that was 24 inches deep. The CFV-2000 was Spartan's Maxi-Vision Series, which offered a windshield that was 31 inches deep and featured a distinctive chrome grille with integral housings for the headlights. Power train options included engines from Detroit Diesel or Cummins, and manual transmissions from Spicer or automatic transmissions from Allison. The bodies were custom-designed to each department's specifications.

One of the mainstays of the FMC commercial offerings in the 1980s was the economy Roughneck line. The noncurved, angular cutouts for the rear wheel wells easily distinguished these units. These no-frill pumpers were largely available in stock at the factory. They were offered in three standard versions, with a midship pump, a midship pump with a separate high-pressure pump, or a front-mount

pump. One of the manufacturing features that lowered the production costs of the Roughneck was panels and doors that were interchangeable from the left side to the right side. The standard fire pump was the 750-gpm FMC Ram Series single-stage pump along with a 750-gallon water tank. One electric rewind booster reel was also standard. Crosslays for preconnects were one of the available options.

The Roughneck line in the mid-1980s was expanded to include a tanker and a top-mount option, in addition to the front and midship models that were already offered. The tanker had the capacity to hold 1,000 or 2,500 gallons of water. When a fire department requested the Ford C-Series tilt-cab, many would require FMC to modify the cab to include a rear canopy with a bench seat for the crew. Other departments kept the cab intact and utilized the rear step for the crew.

FMC still offered the Quick-Attack Pumper Series and used it as a step up from the Roughneck. This was a full Class A pumper available on a commercial chassis, or with a custom chassis. This model met the then-current NFPA 1,900 requirements. Hale and FMC pumps were offered with a 300-gallon water tank that could be upgraded to a 500- or 750 gallon tank. These pumpers were designed with a short-body style that had roughly 96 cubic feet of compartment space, with the option to expand to 138 cubic feet.

FMC also had a line of minipumpers that were built on a pickup truck chassis. These small units had a 250-gpm Hale pump, a 50-gallon booster tank, 58 cubic feet of compartment space, one electric booster reel, and were fabricated out of aluminum. Four-wheel drive was an option.

FMC introduced a new high-end pumper series in 1982. Called the Omega Series, these pumpers were offered on commercial or custom chassis. This was an all-aluminum pumper with a water tank made of polyethylene instead of steel. Conventional side-mount and top-mount panels were standard. The Omega was available with a unique new type of pump controls

This is an example of a Simon Duplex D9400LMFDSC cab with a full-height door. These units differ from most as Duplex used one tall window in the high door. Other builders used two windows that changed the exterior appearance greatly. Saulsbury built the rescue pumper body in 1996 with a 2000-gpm pump and a 500-gallon water tank. The unit belongs to the Willing Hand Hose Company Number 1 of Montoursville, Pennsylvania.

A 1989 FMC Sentinel pumper with a 1250-gpm pump, a 1000-gallon water tank, and a four-door IHC S4900 cab and chassis for Alsip, Illinois.

as an option. Offered as a top-mount, the electronic panel had membrane switches that the operator merely had to depress to control the functions of the pump, and digital readouts replaced the standard round gauges with needles. The panel had a hinged cover that kept it clean when not in use. With the Omega, FMC returned to curved rear wheel wells.

In April 1986, following a labor dispute in Tipton, FMC moved the Fire Apparatus Division to Orlando, Florida, where it already had manufacturing space for one of its other divisions. The first pumper to be constructed in Orlando rolled out in 1986 for Watertown, Connecticut. At the same time, FMC purchased the Van Pelt Fire Truck Company of Oakdale, California, to gain manufacturing facilities for expansion on the West Coast.

Shortly after the move, the new team at FMC introduced the next-generation pumper. The Sentinel was a line of custom and commercial pumpers that featured modular bodies. Since the body would now be built in modular sections instead of one piece, efficiencies in manufacturing would streamline production. The modular construction allowed the chassis to flex and reduce the fatigue on the body, pump, and tank structures. This also was FMC's first design using computer-aided design (CAD)

drawings. Fabrication was from galvanneal steel with the option of choosing aluminum or stainless steel. The bodies had circular rear wheel wells that featured aluminum fenderettes. The standard water tank carried 750 gallons and the standard 1000-gpm pump could be upgraded to as much as 2000 gpm.

Although a fire department could request any chassis, FMC teamed up with Spartan to put together a custom trim package that would be called the FMC Commander. One of the distinctive features of the cab was a wide, black, recessed plastic panel that wrapped around the center of the cab and contained the quad headlight and emergency light housings, as well as a small front grille.

One of the first major orders for the Sentinel Series went to the Baltimore City Fire Department in 1986. These units were built on Spartan LFD Monarch series chassis with 1000-gpm pumps and 750-gallon water tanks.

The Sentinel was available as the Van Pelt Series with three models. The VP I, VP II, and the VP III were all fabricated from 12-gauge galvanneal steel. The VP I was built on a GM Model C7D042 conventional cab chassis with a Detroit 8.2L, 205-horsepower engine and a five-speed

manual transmission. It came standard with a 1000-gpm Ram pump, a 750-gallon water tank, and a price tag of $70,355. The VP II used a Ford C-8000 tilt-cab chassis with a canopy-cab extension. The Caterpillar 3208T 250-horsepower engine with an Allison MT643 four-speed automatic transmission powered it. The unit had a 1250-gpm Ram pump and a 750-gallon booster tank. The price for a VP II was $88,455. The top of the Sentinel line was the VP III. It was built on the FMC Commander custom chassis and powered by a Cummins L10, 300-horsepower engine with an Allison MT647 four-speed automatic transmission. The cab was aluminum, and the same 750-gallon tank was standard, along with a 1500-gpm Ram pump. The cost for this unit was $109,955.

Another series of Sentinel pumpers was fabricated from stainless steel. The SSII and SSIII models offered lifetime warranties on the water tank and stainless-steel body. Both models offered a 1250-gpm Hale pump, a 750-gallon water tank, and a variety of other standard features. The SSII was built on the Ford C-8000 chassis with a tilt-cab that was modified with the extended-crew-cab canopy to provide seating for five. The cab was dressed up with a chrome trim package including fenders, bumper, grille, and grab rails. The SSIII used the FMC Commander custom tilt-cab chassis with seating for six. The engine and transmission matched the specifications for the Van Pelt Series. In 1988, the Commander chassis was also contracted from Pemfab, in addition to Spartan.

Grumman

Howe Fire Apparatus acquired Oren in 1974 and Grumman Emergency Products purchased Howe in 1978. Grumman's facility was in Roanoke, Virginia, which was formerly the home of Oren. Grumman offered a complete line of fire apparatus including mini, midi, and full-size pumpers along with pumper-tankers and aerial devices. Until 1989, most Grumman pumpers were built on such commercial chassis as the

In 1985, FMC introduced this demonstrator unit representing the Omega pumper series. Built on a Spartan two-door Gladiator chassis with a squared cab, the all-aluminum Omega was available on a custom or commercial chassis. One of the new optional features of this unit was a top-mounted electronically controlled pump panel that used membrane switches instead of mechanical levers. The panel had a hinged cover to protect the switches and keep them clean.

In 1990, the Fellowship Fire Company of Mount Laurel, New Jersey, bought this Grumman pumper, featuring a Panther LMFD tilt-cab. HME built the private-label cab and chassis for Grumman between 1989 and 1992.

Ford C Series. It also built on custom chassis by Hendrickson, Pemfab, and Spartan, although the majority of the custom chassis it used were made by Duplex. In 1989, Grumman began to offer the Panther series, which HME produced exclusively for them. This cab and chassis came in several configurations and did not resemble any of the units available to competitors. The Panther was a full tilt-cab style with a standard four-door enclosure (MFD) or an extended option (LMFD). There was also a low-profile version that was largely used with an aerial device.

Grumman offered the Minicat, Attackcat, Wildcat, Tankercat, Customcat, Firecat, and Tigercat models. The "cat" names originated from Grumman's aerospace division, which produced famous military aircraft such as the World War II Hellcat.

The Minicat was a line of quick-attack minipumpers built on pickup truck chassis. These were outfitted with 250-gpm Waterous pumps and carried 250 gallons of water. The Attackcat models were quick-response midipumpers that featured medium-duty commercial chassis with 500 gallons of water and a Waterous pump with a maximum capacity of 1000 gpm.

The Wildcat was Grumman's economy pumper, offering few options on a commercial chassis. Most often this was a stock program with units available for immediate sale. Wildcat units had 750- or 1000-gpm pumps and carried 750 or 1,000 gallons of water. These were most often stocked on Ford C-8000 series chassis or the conventional F-800 chassis.

The Tigercat and Firecat were both full-size custom pumpers that could be purchased on a commercial or custom chassis. The Tigercat was constructed with a modular aluminum body and the Firecat had a modular steel body. These could be ordered with Waterous pumps delivering 750 to 1500 gpm and water tanks as large as 1,000 gallons.

Another Grumman model was the Customcat. As the name suggests, it was a custom pumper designed to meet a specific need. Examples included pumps up to 2000 gpm, water tanks to 2,500 gallons, foam systems, electrical equipment, special plumbing options, one-of-a-kind compartmentation, and specialized chassis. Finally, the Tankercat was Grumman's line of pumper-tankers with up to 3,000 gallons of water delivered by a 2000-gpm pump.

After several years, Grumman reduced its model diversity and simply offered the Firecat in either aluminum or steel, the Minicat, and the Attackcat. Wildcat, Customcat, and Tigercat designations were no longer used.

One could always discern a Grumman pumper from the rear by the trademark taillights that were built into aluminum housings mounted at the corners of the tailboard. Other manufacturers incorporated the taillights into the body. Grumman closed its fire apparatus division in 1992.

Hahn

Hahn Motors of Hamburg, Pennsylvania, produced its first fire apparatus in 1913. It was tapped to aid the war effort during both World War I and World War II by building various other products. It was not until the late 1960s that it concentrated on custom fire apparatus and began turning out some of the finest pumpers available. Although Hahn offered pumpers that were built on commercial chassis, it also pro-

duced its own chassis offering TCM cabs as well as their own cab design. Hahn also fabricated the bodies.

When every truck builder was going to wider cabs in the mid-1980s, Hahn introduced its ultramodern 92-inch-wide Jetcoat model. This cab featured a large windshield area with curved glass that offered the industry a new look differing from the contoured TCM cab in use by so many others. Another distinct aspect of this model was a brushed stainless-steel band that wrapped around the front of the cab. The dual-tiered headlight mountings and engine grille were located in this band, which extended onto both front doors. The cab used short front doors with an exposed step. A four-door design was also available as an option which used modified front doors for the rear enclosure.

When built as a pumper chassis, it was called the HCP Series. The engines used were the Detroit Diesel 6-71T paired with the Allison MT644 automatic transmission, or either the Detroit Diesel 8V71N or

Hahn built this 1250-gpm custom pumper with a two-door, 92-inch-wide Jetcoat custom chassis for the Plymouth Fire Company, Plymouth Township, Pennsylvania, in 1987.

A 1972 Pirsch custom cab-forward pumper is packed up with equipment following a suburban house fire. The curved handrail above the rear-facing jump seats, a Pirsch trademark for many years, would later be instrumental in its demise. The family of an injured volunteer fireman received a multimillion dollar judgment after he fell off a rig while it was moving. The court found Pirsch was negligent for placing the handrail on board, since it encouraged the plaintiff to stand and hold on.

6V92TA paired with the Allison HT740 transmission. Hahn used Hale fire pumps and fabricated its bodies from galvanized steel. Hahn ceased operations in the early 1990s.

Pirsch

Pirsch built its own chassis with a unique custom cab-forward design beginning in the early 1960s. This classic style was extremely popular in the Midwest, the South, and on the East Coast. It offered seating for five and featured a two-piece windshield with flat glass panels that angled away from the center post. The front of the cab below the windows was flat and the rear of the roof over the jump seats had a characteristic cutaway area that was Pirsch's design. This cab was also available in an open design without a roof. For several years after the new cab-forward design went into production, Pirsch was still offering their conventional cab with the engine ahead of the cab as an option.

In 1981, Pirsch built its last custom cab with the distinctive design. From that point forward, the Pirsch custom cab and chassis utilized a TCM Cincinnati cab that had been an available option since 1978. It offered just one model that used the 86-inch-wide contour design. Pirsch dressed them up a little, but for the most part, the distinction that separated them from other manufacturers was gone. Pirsch offered Detroit Diesel or Cummins engines, Hale pumps, and a choice of steel or aluminum for the body. It also built quite a few pumpers on mass-produced commercial chassis, largely the Ford C-8000. Like other builders, Pirsch built the canopy extension and crew seating at the rear of the Ford tilt-cab.

In 1983, Pirsch followed the market trend with the use of the wider 94-inch TCM cab, which it called simply the five-man deluxe canopy cab. Pirsch also offered a fully enclosed four-door cab (LFD) as an option. Many departments requested pumpers with chassis by Spartan, Hendrickson, and Pemfab. Pirsch built very few units on Duplex chassis. Costly litigation marked the final chapter for Pirsch who went out of business in the late 1980s.

Ward '79 Limited

In 1983, Ward '79 began building fire trucks. Its biggest customer was the FDNY, which purchased over 100 units between 1984 and 1989. Ward '79 built the bodies with 12-gauge galvanneal steel and also provided fully enclosed four-door conversions for the Mack CF686FC cabs.

Ward had several different model names when it received the first FDNY contract in 1984. It built 250-gpm/250-gallon minipumpers under the Apollo Series, 500-gpm/500-gallon quick-attack midipumpers under the Mercury Series, and 1000-gpm/500-gallon tilt-cab pumpers under the Vulcan Series. The FDNY pumpers were part of the Fire Mac Series that was saved for FDNY units. The Fire Max Series and the Fire Mac Series featured Mack chassis, such as the CF, R, MC, and MS for other fire departments. Vulcan II was the series name that referred to open canopy cab pumpers with jump seats, while the Jupiter Series covered aerial devices.

Although galvanneal steel was standard, Ward also offered aluminum and stainless steel. Likewise, a 500-gallon tank was standard, but there were options to increase the capacity to 750 or 1,000 gallons.

Ward placed units on both coasts and in many states in between, but was forced to close its doors in 1989.

The 1970s through the 1980s was a tough period for several companies and many contributing factors resulted in a major shakeup and fallout for quite a few fire truck builders. Emergency One, Grumman, and FMC bought out American Eagle, Howe, and Van Pelt, respectively. Some years later, corporate planning and the inability to meet growth and profitability expectations put an end to the fire apparatus divisions of the multinational companies of FMC and Grumman. Among the others that didn't emerge into the 1990s for one reason or another were American LaFrance, Mack, Ward LaFrance, Pirsch, Boyer, Boardman, Crown, Hahn, Young, and Ward '79.

When Pirsch discontinued its own distinctive custom cab-forward design, it began to use TCM cabs with its own trim package on a chassis that it assembled. This 1983 1250-gpm pumper was built for the National Institute of Health in Bethesda, Maryland. It had a unique emergency lighting package for its day, using the four large roof-mounted strobe lights in place of a traditional lightbar.

CHAPTER 3
Pumper Design

Chassis

A pumper is a specialty truck built on a commercial chassis or a custom fire truck chassis. Cement mixers, refuse trucks, utility trucks, and boom trucks are other examples of specialized vehicles that are built to accommodate the industry in which they are used.

There are two ways to begin the design of a pumper. The first centers on a commercial truck chassis that is available to any industry. This includes chassis made by Ford, General Motors, Freightliner, IHC, Peterbilt, and Kenworth, to name some of the more popular companies. A fire department begins by determining how large a vehicle it wants and then shops for a chassis that meets its needs. Gross vehicle weight (GVW), wheelbase, engine size, transmission, and cab design will all play a role in making this decision. Commercial chassis are sometimes available for immediate purchase from a dealer's stock. Each of these chassis will be a good, all-purpose and proven product to serve as a base for the pumper. Since these chassis are readily available for all industries and are mass-produced, there will be cost savings over custom chassis that are produced solely for the fire industry. Another consideration behind many purchases of commercial chassis is the availability of service centers and parts suppliers. If these pumpers are to be incorporated into a large municipal fleet, some purchase managers would prefer to use a commercial chassis that is already in use throughout their fleet with other city

Borrego Springs, California, ordered this pumper from the Western States Company. Built in 1982 on a Spartan CFG-2042 chassis, this pumper incorporated the operator's panel for the 1250-gpm pump into the face of the cab.

Volunteer firemen prepare
to hit a brush fire with a
booster line off this
Seagrave pumper.

departments such as parks, streets, and refuse collection. This simplifies maintenance by consolidating the parts inventories and the training that is required for the mechanics.

The second option that a fire department can pursue is a custom fire truck chassis. Although more costly, these chassis offer many amenities and design features that were incorporated specifically for the fire service, whereas the conventional chassis will require certain modifications or add-ons before they are ready for use. One of the major components of a

custom fire truck chassis that separates it from the commercial chassis is the available cabs. The fire service demands more from the front and rear cab than any other specialized industry. A pumper needs to carry a tremendous amount of equipment and supplies so the firefighters can perform the vast array of duties required of them.

From seating configurations that differ by department to the unique compartments for highly specialized tools, a custom cab offers almost limitless options. There

Before the NFPA mandated fully enclosed cabs, most departments purchased custom pumpers with open, rear-facing jump seats such as those on this unit. Firefighters in this position were only partially shielded from rain, snow, and the cold. In the summer, the engine compartment alongside the seat raised the temperature significantly.

are very few options when it comes to outfitting and changing the cab of a mass-produced commercial truck.

When a pumper is designed, the specifications will take into account the amount of water, hose, personnel, and loose equipment it will carry. The weight of the body and cab will also be considered and this will determine the GVW of the desired chassis. Each type of chassis has limitations on the GVW range that it will accommodate. Shocks, springs, axles, frame rails, the engine, and transmission all need to work together properly to ensure that the truck will hold up and give the department a service life of between 10 and 20 years.

Power Plants

The drivetrain of most fire trucks typically contains the components of a core group of manufacturers. Axles by Rockwell, Eaton, and Meritor are common for pumper chassis. Detroit Diesel (DD), Caterpillar (Cat), and Cummins engines are all used. The standard engines for many years were the Detroit Diesel 6V-92TA and the 8V-92TA along with the Cummins 3116 or 3406 and Cat L10 or NTC400. For the most part, Allison owns the automatic transmission business in the fire industry, offering four, five, and six-speed versions. Fuller and Spicer produce manual transmissions as well as the new Eaton Fuller

One of the first Pierce Lance XLFDSC cabs was outfitted for patient transport in Kent, Washington. This early model was produced before full-height doors that extended into the raised section were used.

CEEMAT automatic transmission. All diesel engines have had to adapt in recent years to conform to changing environmental laws. There was a need for improved fuel economy and to reduce operating costs. Advanced engineering and new materials have produced lighter, more efficient engines that are less costly to maintain.

The 6V and 8V engines were two-stroke engines and could not be modified to meet current emissions requirements under diesel fuel. Today the following engines are designed for the general truck market and can be found powering pumpers. From Detroit Diesel, the four-stroke Series 40, 50, and 60 engines provide a range of 160 to 500 horsepower, complete with their own electronic control systems to monitor all engine functions. Detroit Diesel introduced the turbocharged six-cylinder Series 60 in 1987. It was the first fully integrated heavy-duty diesel

engine with electronic controls. These new engines offer excellent fuel economy when compared with the previous engines. The Series 50 is a four-cylinder engine that shares the same low emissions, excellent fuel consumption, and durability that is found in the Series 60.

These D.D. engines utilize the Electronic Fire Commander (EFC) designed for the fire market. The EFC is a pump controller that combines a pressure sensor governor controller, a display with engine operating criteria, and a monitor for the entire system. This offers the pump operator complete control and monitoring of the engine control system during pumping operations, allowing for the adjustment of the engine idle. The system monitors the temperature, oil pressure, engine rpm, and allows preset rpm settings for operational use.

Cummins offers the ISB, ISC, ISM, and M11+ engines with 175 to 500 horsepower. The 500-horsepower ISM engine is available exclusively for the fire service. The ISB and ISC engines are fully electronic up to 350 horsepower.

Caterpillar makes the CFE and two versions of the C-10, along with two versions of the C-12, with 175 to 455 horsepower available.

It is easy to assume that the more powerful the engine, the better. After all, in the fire service, response time is critical, and more power means faster speeds. The flaw to this theory is that actual driving speed is but one factor in achieving an acceptable response time. More important are preparedness, sufficient manpower, and overall safety for the citizens and firefighters. Nothing is achieved if the engine company is unable to arrive on-scene safely. As a matter of fact, most fire departments have adopted response standard operating procedures (SOPs) that require units to come to a complete stop at controlled intersections where they do not have the right-of-way. Speeding through an intersection against a

red light is extremely dangerous and puts the fire crew and any motorists that cannot hear the sirens at great risk. To assist with this problem, many cities and towns have gone to the expense of purchasing signaling systems that allow emergency vehicles to change the traffic lights in their path, thus eliminating the need to run red lights.

The more powerful rigs with larger power plants are needed to accommodate vehicles with higher GVW or in districts with steep hills. Large water tanks and the equipment that is carried on board will add to the pumper's GVW. Many chassis, both custom and commercial, have restrictions on the actual engines that they can take. As the capacity of the engine increases, the size of the unit grows. Each chassis will have an outline of compatible engines.

Before the newer electronic engines were released, there were fewer changes or engineering considerations required for chassis builders to accommodate the individual engines that a customer might specify. Motor mounts and brackets for each engine, the radiator, and the size of the doghouse were the main considerations that

A split tilt-cab separates at a point that is even with the midpoint of the front axle. The driver's portion tilts forward while the crew area remains stationary, demonstrated by this 1997 Sutphen SMFDSC custom pumper from Weirton, West Virginia. This 1750-gpm pumper also features a brightly colored pump panel and three preconnected crosslays that sit on trays that roll out.

The interior view of an XLFDSC Pierce cab, with seating for six in the crew area plus two up front. Each seat is equipped with special SCBA brackets.

needed to be addressed. Today, the electronic engines share the same needs but also must be fully integrated with the overall electronic system of the vehicle. Each different engine requires engineering changes for the chassis, including particular wiring harnesses to ensure an appropriate interface with the rest of the vehicle. This is why fire truck builders will sometimes restrict certain pumpers to specific engine as a cost saving measure. Older pumpers had gasoline engines with manual transmissions. Today, all motors are diesel and the majority are automatics.

Engine placement is another option. The motor can be mounted in the front of the chassis, in the rear, or in the middle. Moving the motor behind the cab has become a popular option, providing additional interior space and, more importantly, a quieter environment for the firefighters. With the engine mounted in the rear of the chassis, the cab area is extremely quiet.

When deciding which chassis to purchase, a fire department will consider cost, seating and comfort, wheelbase, maneuverability, and engine size. Most often, the commercial, mass-produced chassis will offer the fewest options but will be the most cost-effective. Custom chassis can be fine-tuned to fulfill almost any request by the fire departments. Currently, the cost for a new pumper featuring a commercial chassis and basic features begins at around $100,000. A custom chassis will often add from $40,000 to $60,000 to this price. More features and options can bring the price tag well over $200,000.

Cabs

Safe seating has become a major issue in recent years, in response to NFPA standards and liability concerns. Everyone can remember seeing the engine going down the street with firefighters hanging on while standing on the back step of the vehicle. This tradition of riding the tailboard is gone now. Firefighter injuries from falling off the truck and concerns for protection from the weather have dictated that all personnel be seated with safety belts. Pumpers used to have rear-facing jump seats that were not enclosed; some even lacked roofs overhead. Currently, all personnel in new apparatus are to be inside an enclosed cab with factory-installed safety belts.

Commercial, mass-produced cabs can have two doors with a small crew area that provides seating for two or three people. Four-door commercial cabs offer seating for up to six firefighters. In addition to the two doors for the driver and officer, custom cabs can have two rear-facing doors or two conventional rear doors right behind the front doors. Cabs with rear-facing doors are commonly called short-four-door (SFD) cabs. These will offer seating for four or six people. Cabs with all doors on the sides are medium-four-door (MFD) cabs if the rear doors are cut out to fit over the wheels. Variations that will be discussed in later chapters include short-medium-four-door (SMFD) or long-medium-four-door (LMFD) cabs. The SMFD has a narrower step in the rear doors when compared to the MFD. A LMFD shares the MFD door, but has a longer cab that extends beyond the rear door. A cab with rear doors that are straight and mount totally

behind the wheels is a long-four-door (LFD) cab. Some cabs have raised roofs with enough room for a firefighter to stand while wearing a helmet.

While many cabs are fixed, the majority of new custom units feature tilt-cabs. The tilt-cabs provide two main benefits over the fixed-cab designs. The first is the ease of access to the motor for repair and maintenance. The second benefit is the added space available for the crew and seating. Since the motor is often moved up front between the driver and the officer, the uninterrupted space in the rear allows for more equipment storage and room for the crew to get ready while en route to a call.

The NFPA released guidelines for firefighter safety in relation to the apparatus. Some of these guidelines were mentioned earlier concerning an enclosed cab with seat belts, while others deal with hearing protection and external safety regarding the visibility of the fire apparatus. Reflective striping that completely surrounds the vehicle is a requirement to increase the visibility to passing and approaching motorists. Air horn

This is an example of a pumper squad body. It features full-height compartments with roll-up doors. The rear compartment has an SCBA filling station for an on-board air cascade system in addition to storage for 16 spare bottles. The other compartments have fans, lights, cord reels, and other equipment.

In 1998 when Chicago began purchasing pumpers with shorter bodies and roll-up compartment doors, equipment placement had to be exact or some items would not fit. This shot illustrates the custom layouts and the preparation of the compartments to accommodate all of the equipment, which now includes EMS supplies on many rigs.

and siren placement has been moved from the traditional location on the roof of the cab to a recessed position in the bumper, to minimize the noise that firefighters are subjected to while en route to an emergency. Along these same lines, many fire departments design their pumpers with an intercom system that employs headsets for each person to wear while in the rig. These headsets muffle the external noises and allow for clear communication between all of the occupants to discuss what each will do when they arrive on-scene. The headsets also help the pump operator, who remains with the vehicle while the other firefighters attack the fire. The pump operator can wear the headset to reduce the noise from the engine and pump, since he has to stay at the pump panel for a prolonged period of time.

Some of the companies that produce chassis and cabs for the fire service include American LaFrance, Emergency One, HME, KME, Pierce, Seagrave, Spartan, and Sutphen.

Bodies

Pumper bodies provide many opportunities for customization. Hose storage, compartment size, location of the pump operator's controls, intakes and outlets for hose connections are just a few of the considerations affecting the body's design.

Most pumper bodies have traditionally been fabricated from galvanneal steel using a formed process. In this process, flat panels of steel are cut to match the design using a large press. The panels are then welded together and formed into the appropriate shapes that become the body and compartments. This is done piece by piece onto the already completed chassis. The next most abundant material for fabricating pumper bodies is aluminum. Aluminum bodies can also be formed, though many are built in modules with extrusions, commonly referred to as modular extruded aluminum bodies.

Aluminum was introduced as a lighter-weight material that was resistant to corrosion. The lighter weight would allow a lower overall GVW, allowing fire departments to carry more water and equipment. Departments that were exposed to road salt and other corrosive agents were constantly battling rust on their apparatus. Aluminum was intended to prolong the life of fire apparatus in these environments.

While formed bodies are built as a complete unit onto the chassis, a modular body is built in separate sections. Each of these sections or modules can be built simultaneously. This can be accomplished at the same time that the chassis is being built. When the chassis and body modules are completed, they can be assembled, producing the finished unit. Modular construction is quicker and is better suited to repair and reconstruction

This 1992 Pierce (SFD) rear door Dash pumper from Wading River, New York, is prepared for the rapid deployment of LDH (large-diameter hose). They have two different sizes, one with a gated Y-valve already attached. The unit also features high-side top hinging compartments on both sides, a hydraulic ladder rack, top-mounted pump panel, and a rear booster reel.

in the event of an accident. Emergency One pioneered the modular body design in the fire service. Today, many companies offer this type of construction.

When Emergency One started building bodies from aluminum, it used extrusions for strength. In addition to Emergency One, Ferrara, Luverne, and Central States currently offer extruded aluminum bodies. An extrusion is made of aluminum alloys that are forced through a die to form a specific structural shape. This becomes a structural member for a particular part of the cab or body. The die can be designed to form any shape to place a greater thickness of material at strategic locations in the extrusion. The greater thickness accommodates the force experienced when the extrusion is subjected to load during use. Other metals do not have the same properties as aluminum, which allow it to be formed into the different types of extrusions. After the substructure of extrusions is welded into place, aluminum smooth plate is welded over the extrusions to form the sides, top, and bottom of the body and compartments.

In the early 1970s, most pumper bodies featured two external compartments on each side of the rig. These were low compartments that were on either side of the wheel wells. Ground ladders were mounted above the compartments on the passenger side, while the driver's side either had nothing or sections of hard suction hose for drafting. Many volunteer departments added racks above the hard suction hose and ladders to store boots, coats, and helmets for the firefighters. When the alarm sounded, someone was responsible for bringing the pumper to the fire scene while the rest of the volunteers responded in their own vehicles. Once on the scene, they would grab gear off the pumper and then go to work.

The next trend in body designs included additional compartments on the driver's side. These were called high-side compartments and ran from the pump panel to the rear of the body. Hard suction hoses were often mounted above these compartments, above the ground ladders on the other side, or in both places. These new compartments more than doubled the available storage space for equipment. Very often, one of these was used for self-contained breathing apparatus (SCBA). When the NFPA and OSHA mandated that firefighters use air masks on a regular basis, companies that manufactured the seats for the cabs began to build SCBA storage directly into the seat back. This meant that firefighters could get into their SCBAs while en route to a fire scene and exit the rig ready for action.

The high-side compartments are offered in several varieties. One style has vertically

Here is an example of a pumper with custom equipment storage. Notice the varnished wood boards for the tool mounting. The top compartments are hinged to open upward and out of the way, and this department opted for a full-height rear compartment to mount SCBA packs, fire extinguishers, and a large fan.

hinged doors that open to the side. These have stainless-steel door hold-open springs that lock into place when the doors are fully opened. In order to close the door, a fire-fighter first has to push the spring in, which allows the door to swing closed. An alternative door style, called spring-loaded doors opens upward. This allows an unobstructed walk along the side of the pumper while the compartment doors are open. These doors also offer protection from the rain for anyone standing underneath them.

Regardless of the hinging method, pumper bodies are offered with two large compartments or three smaller compartments depending on the preferences of the purchasing department.

Door construction is either lap-type or flush. Flush doors are cut to fit the opening exactly without protruding from the body. Lap doors are mounted on the outside of the body and overlap the opening on all sides. Each style is fitted with rubber gaskets to protect the equipment inside the compartment.

Most pumper bodies also offer some method of deflecting rain at the top of the compartment structure to prevent water from entering the compartments.

One other type of compartment door has emerged, largely due to European influences. Instead of a hinged metal door, shutter-type roll-up doors have gained popularity in the United States. When open, these doors do not protrude beyond the sides of the body, since they roll up within the compartment. Some departments prefer these doors to prevent the problems that occur when a spring-loaded hinged door is not properly latched and opens by itself when it should not. This happens when a rig is either driving down the street or, most often, when the rig is leaving quarters. When a door pops open as the rig drives out of the fire station, the frame of the apparatus bay door can shear off the door. Although this may sound unlikely, it is a common occurrence in the fire service.

Fashioned after an FDNY design, the fire company chose to have a canvas cover over the hose bed area. Ground ladder storage is located here since the rig has high-side compartments on both sides. Most of the bed is filled with LDH for supply, but there are also two preconnects on the left as well as larger hose for attack lines on the right.

Sometime after high-side compartments were introduced on the driver's side, pumpers began to emerge with high-sides on the officer's side also. This provides a significant increase in storage space, but requires the ground ladders to be moved. The most common spot for the ladders is on a hydraulic rack that places the ladders above the compartments on the officer's side. Brackets for the ladder rack bring the ladders down along the side of the pumper, in front of the compartments. This allows firefighters to reach the ladders and remove them for use.

As early as the 1940s, alternative ladder storage was available in a stationary rack above the hose bed. This moved the ladders out of the way, but was cumbersome when it came time to use the ladders.

Another storage method implemented by several fire truck builders places the ground ladders in a storage compartment that is accessible from the rear of the pumper. Usually incorporated into the side of the hose bed, some designs place the ladders below the hose bed with a special compartment that goes through the water tank. This provides for ground ladder access that is similar to many styles of aerial trucks.

Fire hose is made in various diameters for different uses. Hoses that measure 1 1/2 to 2 1/2 inches in diameter are referred to as attack lines, while larger sizes are supply lines. Quite simply, supply lines are responsible for the water supply coming to the pumper or to supply a group of attack lines. Attack lines are used by the firefighters to hit the fire. Each fire department has its own hose complement that fits its SOPs, although the NFPA requires a minimum of 400 feet of attack line and 1,200 feet of supply line on every Class A-rated pumper.

This department chose to use a full-height compartment to hold a complete set of hydraulic rescue tools. The reels will have cords for quick connections to the tools for use near the rig; otherwise the portable generator on the bottom can be carried anywhere it is needed.

Often, this is used as a starting point for what eventually makes up the total hose complement per unit.

Cities or towns with a good water supply and fire hydrants located throughout their district may require less supply line because they won't have to rely on long hose lays. Older cities may carry larger quantities of supply hose to connect to hydrants farther away so that they use more than one water main at a large fire. If all the pumpers are using the same water main, the available pressure may be reduced. Supply lines today are most often 4- and 5-inch diameter hose.

All of the hose is carefully packed into the rear hose bed or into the different preconnected beds that can be at the rear or midship. Every department has its own preferred way of packing the hose to optimize SOPs. With the exception of the diameter, all hose used to look identical. Currently, hose lines are available in a number of different colors to customize a pumper. Each preconnected line, for example, can correspond to the color-coded gauges on the pump panel that control them. Several years ago, all hose had to be dried after it was used to prevent mildew.

After a fire, the hose was rolled up and placed on the tailboard for the trip back to the fire station. Once there, the hose would be hung in a hose tower to dry to prevent mildew. Then the hose missing from the pumper would be replaced with spare hose. Only then would the pumper be declared back in service and ready to respond to the next emergency.

Modern hose no longer needs to be dried. After the fire, the hose is merely re-loaded into the rear hose bed or preconnect beds and readied again for service.

Water tanks range from 500 to 1,500 gallons and may be supplemented by one or two separate tanks for foam. The tank can be made of aluminum, steel, or plastic and have distinct shapes that allow the body's compartments to be built around it. On the top of the pumper, there is an access hatch for filling the water tank and the foam tank if the pumper has one.

Pumps

The pump is rated in gpm and can provide outputs from 750 to 2,000 gpm. Similar to the motor, the pump can have several different mounting positions. The most common pump location is in the middle, or midship. Pumps are being mounted at the rear or, in rare instances, in the front of the unit. The pump is generally not visible from the outside of the vehicle.

The pump operator's panel, or pump panel as it is called in the fire service, is where the engineer stands to send water through the hose lines and shut it off on command. Placement of the pump panel can be on the front of the cab, inside the cab, at the rear of the pumper, or most often just behind the cab where the body begins. More than half of the pump panels are on the side of the unit, requiring the operator to stand next to the vehicle. And many are on top of the rig, accessible from a passageway that spans the width of the body.

The most common spot to find the control panel is on the driver's side of the body, just behind the cab. At a side-mounted panel, the operator often connects supply or attack lines to pipe connectors or "ports" that are built into the panel. This allows the operator access to equipment stored in the compartments and to a radio. The panel gives the operator the ability to monitor and adjust the output of water to the firefighters using the hoses. If the fire is behind the pumper, often the attack lines will come off the back of the unit and the water supply line can be connected to the side or to an intake on the front bumper. The valve controls on a side-mount panel are most often in the form of levers that are pulled out to initiate the flow of water and pushed back in to shut down the hoses. These are called push/pull rods with T-handles.

Another very popular spot for the operator's panel is on top of the unit. Here, the operator climbs up to a walkway built behind the cab that allows access to the other side of the pumper. This is called a top-mounted console, and the operator is elevated from the street with the ability to see what is happening on all sides of the pumper. Whereas the operator cannot see the other side of the pumper with a side-mounted console, the top-mounted version allows him or her to better keep track of where the lines are, in addition to where the firefighters are, to provide assistance when it is needed. This position also puts the operator out of harm's way when working at an accident scene on a busy highway or street.

A Seagrave pump panel for a pumper with a 1500-gpm pump that carries 500 gallons of water plus two 30-gallon foam tanks. The long vertical tube on the right side of the panel is a gauge to monitor the level of water in the tank. Some departments prefer a system with lights that monitor the level in quarter-tank increments.

Here is a unit with a top mount control panel. The full-width walkway provides work space for the operator. This rig has two preconnects and three speed lays. The speed lays fill the trays below the pump panel. Each line is a different color that matches the color-coding on the pump panel levers and gauges.

The side-mounted panel requires the operator to stand in the street, which can be extremely dangerous. A mechanical top-mounted panel itself consists of throttles, levers, and gauges to monitor water pressure. The valve controls here are levers that pivot back and forth. The intakes and discharges are still located on the sides of the pumper.

A variation on the top-mounted pump panel puts the panel inside an extended and raised cab enclosure (LFDSC or XLFDSC). This allows for all of the advantages of the exterior top-mounted console with the addition of providing a climate-controlled environment for the operator. The operator can work within an air-conditioned chamber in the extreme heat of summer and a heated space in the winter. While those manning the hoses may get hot, it's good to have the pump operator protected to ensure the vital flow of water goes uninterrupted.

There is one other hybrid configuration for the pump panel called a top-side panel. Here, the controls are located in a position above the street level, requiring the operator to stand on a raised platform. Unlike a top-mounted panel, though, there is not a walkway extending the entire width of the vehicle. Either the operator stands facing the opposite side of the vehicle, or toward the rear. The panel is more compact than most (about half the size of a top-mount console) and the operator must remain in one place. This allows the operator a better view of the entire scene than with a side-mount panel, without requiring the extra body length of a full top-mount console.

One recent trend places the pump panel on the pumper's side at the rear of the body instead of midship. Some position the panel on the curbside to keep the operator out of traffic and often closer to the action. Still another design places the controls on the rear of the unit. A third design that is not at all common these days had the operator's controls located on an extended front bumper, referred to as a front-mounted pump.

Depending on the design of the pumper, a pump panel can be fairly plain and simple, or extremely complex and customized. Some pumps have the capacity to handle more hand lines and will have additional discharges to accommodate them. Each discharge requires a gauge to monitor the water pressure in pounds per square inch, a lever to open and close the pipe allowing for the flow of water to commence or terminate, and a label identifying the discharge's location on the pumper. Modern pumpers are built with a color-coding to eliminate any confusion regarding which discharge is being used. The officer can simply call for the "blue inch-and-three-quarter line" to be charged, and the operator knows precisely where to go. The label under the gauge matches the label under the appropriate discharge wherever it is located on the vehicle. Every pump panel has a radio to allow for communications between the pump operator and the firefighters manning the attack lines. In some cases, it is a conventional radio microphone or a telephone-type handset so the pump operator can cradle it close to his

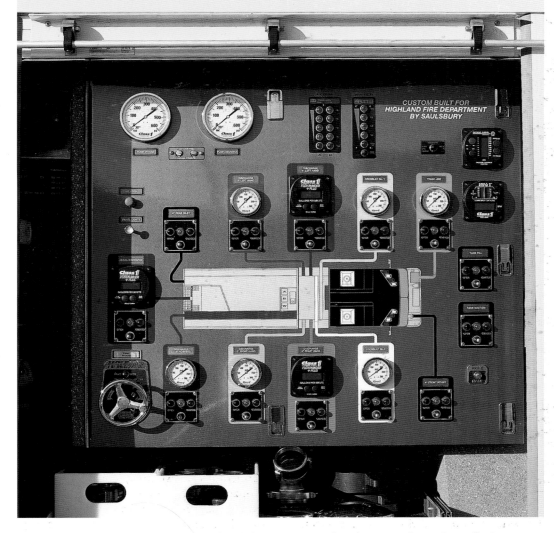

Saulsbury offers this unique control panel that it calls a diagrammatic panel. A detailed view of the pumper from the top allows the operator to trace each discharge by location and color to the appropriate gauges and electronic valve controls. At the top are tank fill indicators that use a series of lights to monitor the tank levels.

ear to shield the communications from the noises of the pump. As mentioned earlier, many departments now use a headset with a hands free microphone for added mobility.

FMC introduced a pump panel in the early 1980s that was fully electronic and used touch-sensitive membrane switches. Currently, Saulsbury makes a very modernistic operator's panel that it calls its "Diagrammatic" pump panel system. This incorporates hydraulic, electric, or manually operated valves into a panel that includes a drawing of the pumper as seen from the top. Each discharge and intake port is color-coded and has an illustration that leads to the appropriate controls. The diagram is detailed to include all of the features of that particular unit as seen from above.

Analog gauges have also changed over the years. Prior to 1991, gauges were subject

to condensation and random fluctuations that would interfere with the operator's ability to accurately deliver the appropriate amount of pressure to the firefighters manning the line. For instance, if the pumper was driven out of a warm fire station into an environment that was colder, condensation had a tendency to form, clouding the gauge and making it difficult to read the pressure. Additionally, needles had a tendency to bounce back and forth with a fluctuation of between 20 and 30 pounds on the dial. To combat these problems, gauges with needles are now produced with a liquid inside the gauge. A combination of glycerin and silicone slows down the movement of the needle, resulting in a more accurate reading. A small device called a snubber controls the amount of liquid going to each gauge. A bourdon tube in each gauge attaches to a

A top-mounted operator's control panel on an E-One pumper. In place of analog gauges, this unit features electronic readouts for each discharge.

Four 1 1/2-inch attack lines have been charged for this fire in addition to the booster line from the reel on top. Perhaps the firefighters thought they could handle the fire with this line before it got out of hand.

hook that goes to a gear which turns the needle. Introducing air or water pressure into the gauge stiffens the bourdon tube and allows it to accurately refleet the reading.

To simplify some of the gauge concerns and to offer a more accurate reading for each port, electronic gauges are also offered with an LED digital display. This eliminates all of the guesswork. These digital gauges can also allow the operator to monitor the water flow in gpm, in addition to the pressure in psi. These new gauges eliminate the need for the operator to calculate the flow at the nozzle by incorporating distance and friction loss. If the nozzle man wants 90 gpm, this becomes a simple adjustment.

Other gauges and readouts on the control panel tell the operator what the level is in the pumper's water or foam tank. These tank level gauges can be digital, analog, or a series of lights that indicate the level from full to empty in quarter-capacity increments. Recently, departments have began to design their pumpers with four large lights, each a different color, that are mounted on the exterior of the cab. These correspond with the four lights on the operator's panel to allow the firefighters to see the tank level from a distance. This comes in handy for a department that has minimal manpower

and may not be able to assign someone to remain at the pump panel when the unit arrives on-scene. They can monitor the tank level from a distance while they are working. This allows them to know what their status is while awaiting the arrival of an additional unit that will supplement their water supply.

Pump operation involves getting water through the pump and opening valves to allow water to flow through to the hose lines. The engine rpm regulates the amount of water that is discharged. To get water flowing out of the pump, the operator has to open a valve within the pump. This can be accomplished in three different ways. The first involves pulling on a handle that is attached to the gate valve inside the discharge pipe. The second method involves a lever that is pulled to one side or the other,

depending on the layout of the pump panel. Again, this is attached to the gate valve. The third method is handled electronically with a touch-sensitive switch on the operator's panel instead of using a mechanical design. The outcome is the same with any of the three methods.

Other Attributes

Other equipment that is standard on most pumpers includes scene lighting. This can be in the form of permanent floodlights that are mounted to the side of the body, removable lights that are powered from an onboard generator, directional floodlights that can be swiveled and raised, or large roof-mounted light towers that are remote-controlled. One of the pump operator's responsibilities at a fire scene is to provide illumination at a nighttime incident to ensure

A close-up view of the rear crew area that was added by Pierce to a Ford C Series cab. Pierce also fabricated the lower compartment for storing a section of LDH and attack lines.

This is an interior view of a Pierce Dash 2000 cab with a raised roof. Each seat is equipped with storage brackets for an SCBA pack, and every person has a headset for communication within the cab.

is affixed to a wood panel coated with several coats of a high-gloss varnish. This board is then mounted to the rear wall of the compartment and each fitting, tool, or nozzle has a permanent home that is easily accessible at an emergency.

The newer rescue-style pumpers with deep compartments are outfitted with all of the modern hydraulic rescue tools, mounted cord reels, generators, and other equipment that can be used by any firefighter that needs them. Space around the wheel wells that might otherwise be wasted is fitted with storage for spare air cylinders or removable wheel chocks which, when placed around the wheels, will prevent the unit from rolling. Inside door panels can also accommodate tool mounting.

Depending on the department, the equipment carried on a pumper can vary. Some of the items that are on all pumpers are SCBA, spare bottles for each SCBA on board, axes, hand tools, pike poles, ground ladders, an attic ladder, a collapsible ladder, supply hose, attack hose, nozzles for the attack lines, first aid supplies, and fittings and couplings to attach a supply line to a hydrant. EMS or paramedic engines will carry medical supplies and equipment beyond the basic supplies that are carried on every pumper.

One facet of the engine, which used to be very popular, is the booster line. Also called a red line, the booster is a rigid rubber hose that winds around a large reel. It is easy to pull and use, and very simple to rewind without much effort. Allowing for a maximum of perhaps 90 gpm, this line is ideal for trash fires and other small fires. Despite the easy-to-use features, many departments have eliminated the booster lines from their rigs. This is due in large part to firefighters who were using the red lines in the wrong situations. Since they are so easy to operate, they were regularly used for fires that should have had a larger diameter attack line with a 300 gpm capacity. Firefighters were incurring injuries because they did not use the appropriate tool for the task.

Most pumpers will also have the means to deliver large volumes of water on a fire from a safe distance when the firefight becomes purely defensive. This master stream

firefighter safety and to aid them while performing their jobs.

Equipment storage and placement can be simple, complex, or a true art form, depending on those responsible for laying out the pumper. Many departments use standard compartments and simply place most of their equipment inside, either sitting directly on the floors, or in storage containers. Others design each compartment around the equipment that will be placed within. Using painstaking preparations, every inch of space is utilized. Tools, supplies, and equipment are meticulously mounted into the compartments on special tool boards, slide-out shelving, or directly to the metal sides. Traditionally, the equipment to be mounted can be in the form of a portable deluge gun, which is fed by large-diameter hose and sits on the ground. Another master stream device is a rig-mounted deck gun attached to a discharge that can be controlled directly from the operator's panel. Some of these are permanently mounted, while others can be used on top of the rig or removed and placed in the street for ground-level work.

In addition to water, foam is also used to control fire in many situations. Hazardous chemical situations are typically treated with foam, but foam has also become common for fighting conventional structure fires. A pumper can utilize foam by tapping into a five-gallon can of foam concentrate with an eductor that injects the foam with water while using a conventional attack line. Other pumpers have on-board foam tanks or cells, which can be tapped directly for application by a foam system that was installed with the water pump. This will automatically mix the foam concentrate with the water inside the pump before discharging the solution through the hose line.

One common system type is a Compressed Air Foam System (CAFS), which mixes the foam solution with compressed air to produce a tightly packed and dense foam mixture that is applied through an attack line. Compressed air foam streams, which are partially filled with air, are projected farther than water streams and produce lighter hoselines that are easier to maneuver.

Since compressed air foam puts out fire four to five times faster than water, it is a more efficient use of the available water supply. It causes less property damage and minimizes firefighter fatigue. This may be most beneficial to rural fire departments that do not have an adequate water supply and manpower. The downside is largely the expense of the foam as opposed to the zero cost of the water. Some fire departments charge the insurance companies for the foam.

Water Supply

Every pumper carries a variety of equipment that allows the operator to make a connection for a continuous water supply. These supplies are generally located on the rig where the pump operator can get at

them quickly. One method involves a section of soft, pliable, large-diameter hose that the driver can attach to a fire hydrant. Depending on the design of the pumper, this hose is commonly stored in a recessed area on the front bumper or directly under the pump panel near the large intake port. These are used when the pumper is parked close to a fire hydrant.

Hard suction hose is also used by many departments for connecting to a fire hydrant, or more commonly, for drafting operations from a stationary water source that has to be pulled into the pump using suction. Hard suction hose is mounted above the high-side compartments, above the ground ladders, in place of the high-side compartment, or in the rear hose bed.

If the pumper is not positioned close to the hydrant, large-diameter supply hose will be used from the rear hose bed. Any length is possible, since all of the hose is coupled together and the pumper will generally carry from 400 to 1,000 feet of this hose.

Instead of four rear-facing seats, some departments replace the center seats with an additional storage compartment, often to accommodate medical supplies.

CHAPTER 4
Trucks and Firefighters in Action

The pumper driver goes by any one of several titles, depending on the area of the country. On the East Coast, the driver is referred to as the chauffeur. In the Midwest as well as the West Coast, the driver is the engineer or pump operator. In many departments, this position is a promotion from firefighter with greater pay and benefits. Other departments rotate personnel between the various engine company positions based on the cross training they have received. Regardless, this person is responsible for making sure that the firefighters advancing a hose on the fire have an adequate and uninterrupted water supply. This is not only vital to extinguish the fire, but to protect the attack crew and other firefighters from the heat and flames.

The driver is responsible first and foremost for getting the company to the incident quickly and safely. One often overlooked aspect of the driver's duties is a thorough familiarity with the response district (first due area). This includes street names, locations, the direction of traffic flow, and the numbered blocks to go directly to an exact address. This is vital to get the company to an incident in the shortest time.

In years past, fire trucks would always be seen heading to every call with lights going, sirens blaring, and moving full speed, regardless of the type of call. The fire service saw plenty of response-related motor vehicle

Chicago Engine 43 uses its 1996 HME SFO Luverne pumper at an extra alarm fire on the city's West Side. Another pumper and two aerials are also visible working in the background. Behind engine 43, a gated Y-adapter in the street supplies an attack line.

The pump operator does not need to wear full protective gear when he remains with the rig. Here, he has one large-diameter line bringing water into the pump, and he is monitoring two small attack lines.

accidents. Almost as relevant as the accident cost in terms of personal injury and vehicular damage, is the legal liability that follows any accident, especially one involving a municipal vehicle.

Today, fire departments have implemented SOPs to regulate the manner in which a unit is allowed to respond. Non-life-threatening emergencies in many departments have been downgraded to nonemergency response status. Some call it running cold, others refer to this as silent, quiet, or noncode. These responses require the apparatus driver to obey all traffic laws including speed limits, and other traffic signs and lights.

This policy is extended in some cases to responses to automatic fire alarms (AFA). Either everyone runs cold, or the initial due "still" company runs hot, while the second due companies run cold. Regardless of the exact SOP, changes have occurred throughout the country to limit accidents and excessive wear on the vehicles. The St. Louis, Missouri,

Fire Department has gone so far as to implement a policy for all responses that require lights and sirens to remain within the posted speed limits.

Drivers also need to have knowledge concerning the placement of hydrants in their still district, again in an effort to minimize the time it takes to secure an uninterrupted continuous water supply. If they need to find a hydrant before proceeding to the fire building, the driver has to know where to look for it. Likewise, after stopping at the fire, the driver must locate the nearest hydrant for a reverse lay.

The operation proceeds as follows. Whether the department implements a reverse or forward lay (discussed below), they must catch a hydrant for a continuous water supply. Since a pumper carries water in a tank, this will be used to sustain the initial attack while the hydrant connection is made. An average capacity for the nozzle at the end of the hose is 200 gpm. A water tank that holds 500 gallons will then sustain a 2 1/2-minute attack before the water supply is exhausted. Likewise, a 1,000-gallon tank will permit up to 5 minutes of attack. During this brief time, the engineer must get the water supply flowing from the hydrant into the pump. The number of people involved depends on the type of lay used to get to the hydrant. A firefighter will assist the engineer with a forward lay, while the engineer will handle a reverse lay by himself.

If a fire department's SOP calls for using the preconnected attack lines, they will perform a forward lay to position the pumper in front of the fire building. The supply line will be large-diameter hose and, providing that the hydrant has adequate pressure, they will be ready to go. If the department uses a smaller diameter supply line or if the hydrant has poor pressure, then the next pumper to arrive will have to intervene at the hydrant and literally push the water to the first engine. This is called in-line pumping, where the water source is pumped from one pumper to another. Both pump operators are required to stay with their rigs for in-line pumping.

The forward lay consists of catching a hydrant while approaching the fire. Here, the pumper will drop a firefighter off at the hydrant who will grab the end of the supply line that is packed in the rear hose bed. The firefighter wraps the hose around the hydrant and signals for the driver to go. The pumper then proceeds to the front of the fire building while large-diameter hose is pulled off the pumper, dropping into the street. When the rig stops, the driver performs a series of actions while the officer and the remaining firefighter, assuming a crew of four, pull a preconnected attack line off the rig. The driver puts the transmission into neutral, sets the parking brake, switches the pump transmission into the pump mode, and then moves the rig's transmission from neutral into drive. At this point, the transmission is turning the pump instead of the rear wheels of the rig. The same horsepower that is available to drive the rig is now ready to power the pump.

The reverse lay is another approach to placement of the pumper and establishing the water supply. Departments that use this method do not use preconnected attack lines. The driver will approach the fire building and stop while the crew jumps off the rig. Firefighters will grab an attack line off the rig and start advancing it to the fire building. The driver estimates the number of hose lengths that will be needed to reach the fire and pulls them off the rig. Then the driver proceeds past the building to the nearest hydrant, laying hose as he goes. As the attack crew is advancing into the building, the driver positions the pumper at the hydrant and makes the connection. Since this operation is done very quickly in most cases, the hydrant connection is made by the time the crew calls for water.

Departments that place their pumpers at the hydrant by using a reverse lay often use the front intake because they drive the pumper right to the hydrant. This also frees up space at the pump panel, allowing the operator totally unrestricted access. This technique is a quicker hook-up for the pump operator, since the front intake line is preconnected to the intake port on many pumpers. The reverse lay also frees up the hydrant man, who is required to wait at the hydrant during a forward lay.

The driver pulls a lever marked "tank to pump." This allows the tank water to

flow through the pump. As this occurs, the pump discharge pressure increases. A gauge monitors this. Next, the operator needs to throttle up the pump to the desired pressure for the attack line that is going to be used. In the case of a preconnect, the length of the line is predetermined by the amount of hose that was packed into the crosslay or rear bed. Many departments operate with 100 pounds of pressure at the nozzle for a 125-gpm flow. In order to achieve this pressure, the operator needs to know the effects of friction loss caused by the insides of the hose contacting the water running through it. This friction reduces the pressure of the water traveling through the hose on its way to the nozzle. Friction loss is affected by the distance traveled, the diameter of the hose, and whether the line is on level ground or traveling up stairs to an upper floor. Rules of thumb are applied to these calculations in addition to various aspects of physics with known formulas.

Distance of an attack line translates into friction loss of 15 pounds per 100 feet of line on level ground. An additional 5 pounds is lost per floor that the line travels up stairs. In order for the pump operator to achieve 100 pounds of pressure at the nozzle for a 200-foot preconnected 1 3/4-inch line

Two 1 3/4-inch preconnects are working off this Pierce Arrow pumper. Note that the front door is curved where it meets the wheel well, unlike earlier models that were straight. Equipment lying on the ground is the responsibility of the pump operator, as is anything that was removed from the open compartments.

The engineer of this Pierce Saber pumper pulled right up to a hydrant and used his front intake port. He is providing a single supply line to another unit that is working closer to the fire scene.

This 1989 Seagrave HB Series pumper tapped a hydrant with two large-diameter lines. He is pumping in-line to another unit that is closer to the fire scene where no hydrant is available. He is using the front intake and driver's side intake, while discharging through a large-diameter line from the officer's side.

going into the front door of a house, he needs to throttle the pump to 130 pounds on the discharge gauge.

As he throttles the pump to 130 pounds, the attack line is being dragged into the fire building. When the signal is given from the hose man to charge the line with water, the driver opens the discharge valve that corresponds to the discharge port where the hose line is attached. Depending on the design of the pump panel, this is achieved by pulling a handle straight out from the panel, activating an electronic

switch, or by throwing a lever, accomplishing the same task. As the valve is opened, a gate within the pump is opened, allowing water to flow where the pump operator is directing it, in this case into the attack line.

At this point, the attack company generally has between 2 1/2 and 5 minutes worth of water to hit the fire while protecting themselves. An experienced firefighter will not initially open the nozzle to the full capacity unless he or she is sure that the fire can be extinguished quickly. If the hydrant connection is not made in a matter of minutes, the attack

Chicago Engine 55's 1980 E-One Sentry III pumper has a Ford C Series cab and chassis with an added canopy area for the firefighters. It is using the front intake and supplying two attack lines. In the background, an E-One Tower Ladder Number 21 is standing by after the battalion chief has struck out the fire.

The fog nozzles are set on straight streams to achieve maximum reach from these two attack lines. The rig is a 1997 Seagrave TB60DA XLFDSC pumper with a 1750-gpm pump, 500-gallon water tank, and a 30-gallon foam tank.

crew will be in an unprotected position where they could be seriously burned.

After charging the attack line, and at the same time the company begins to hit the fire, the pump operator needs to hook up the supply to continue the firefight before the attack crew notices a loss of pressure. He has the same 2 1/2 to 5 minutes to complete this task. The pump operator runs to the rear of the rig where the large-diameter supply line is hanging off, still attached to the hose that was not pulled off the rig. He finds a coupling to separate the line in the street from the hose still in the bed, and takes it to the nearest intake port to get the water into the pump. Intakes that go directly to the pump may be located at the rear of the rig, on the front bumper, or on either side of the rig.

In the case of the forward lay, the firefighter that remained at the hydrant will use a hydrant wrench to remove the cover so he can attach his end of the supply line to the hydrant at the same time that these other operations are being performed. After coupling his end of

the supply line to an intake port, the pump operator signals or calls to the firefighter waiting at the hydrant to charge the line. The hydrant valve is then opened, sending water charging down the line toward the pumper. Before this water is introduced into the pump, the air in the line must be released using a bleeder between the hose coupling and the pump itself.

The operator then slowly opens the intake port, while at the same time adjusting the throttle down to maintain the pressure at the nozzle so he does not overcome the attack crew with the increased pressure. This process ends when the intake port is fully opened.

If the attack crew is concerned that they may exhaust the tank water before the hydrant water is available, the nozzle man might feather the nozzle down to conserve water and maintain their protection from the heat.

Now that the continuous water supply has been established, the operator closes the

A 1972 Darley pumper on a Ford C900 cab and chassis with full-height compartments sits working at a winter fire. Since this department did not have Darley add a crew area to the rear of the cab, it can only seat a crew of three across the front.

Firefighters rest alongside their American LaFrance Pioneer pumper after a house fire. One attack line was used from a rear discharge.

After executing reverse lays, two of Chicago's engines are supplying water to units working at a fire on the city's North Side. Engine 106 is a 1985 E-One Hurricane pumper and Engine 22 is a 1992 Luverne pumper with a Spartan MFD Diamond cab and chassis. Engine 106 is using a side intake while Engine 22 is using the front intake.

tank-to-pump valve. When he has the opportunity, he will open the tank-fill valve to replenish the on-board water supply. He knows when the tank is full either by monitoring the tank gauge or when he notices the water overflowing the tank and gushing out beneath the pumper.

The hydrant man at this point will either pull another line or assist the attack company that has already advanced a line into the structure. If additional lines are pulled off the first engine, the procedure to charge the line with water is similar to the initial line with one difference. As the discharge gate is opened slowly on the new line, the operator needs to adjust the throttle upward, so the initial attack line does not experience a loss of pressure. When both lines are at the desired pressure, the pump operator then will set the relief valve to protect each attack company from excess pressure when the other shuts down its nozzle. Without the relief valve, all the pressure from the first line will be directed to the second line when the nozzle is shut down on the first line.

Regardless of the type of hoselay, the pump operator will monitor the pump panel to ensure adequate pressure for the attack lines and to make adjustments to each that may be called for by the individual firefighters. He will also assist the firefighters who need tools or equipment that are stored on the pumper as well as help to replace empty SCBA bottles from a firefighter's harness.

Some departments require that the pump operator remain with the vehicle at all times in the event that the rig is needed in the firefight. Others will utilize the driver as part of the engine company when it is apparent that the vehicle will not be used to pump water.

Departments that utilize the reverse lay can encounter difficulties if the engine arrives after the aerial truck is in position. Since the street may be impassable due to the other apparatus, the driver has two options. The first is to pull straight in and find the closest hydrant. This requires the attack lines to be pulled off the rig and stretched to the fire scene. The second and often preferred alternative is for the driver

to back the engine down the street until he reaches the other apparatus. At this point, he can dump his hose and proceed forward to the hydrant at the end of the block, implementing the reverse lay.

The manner in which the supply line is attached to the hydrant varies by department and by the type of hydrant. In the areas of the country that experience freezing conditions, the style of hydrant used is called a dry barrel. In this type of hydrant, the gate that opens and closes the water flow is located underground, below the freeze line. When the hydrant is opened, water rushes up to fill the hydrant and find whichever port or ports are open. When the gate is closed, a relief drain that is located below the freeze line allows the excess water from the barrel to drain below the surface to avoid a frozen hydrant that is inoperable during an emergency.

Since the barrel is full of pressure once the gate is opened, it is not possible to tap this hydrant with a second supply line without first closing the gate and shutting the hydrant down. To get around this scenario, departments will attach a gated Y-valve to the hydrant coupling before attaching the large-diameter supply line to it. This new valve has two ports for supply lines that have individually controlled gates. Anytime after the hydrant is flowing water, a firefighter or pump operator can attach an additional large-diameter supply line to the new valve securing additional water for the attack pumper or another unit. When the new line is attached, it is just a matter of opening the gate on the other side of the Y-valve.

Locations that do not experience ground freezing use wet barrel fire hydrants. These units always have water in the barrel and have individually controlled ports. The supply line is attached to a port and the gate valve is then opened to that port only. Additional lines can be attached at any time without interrupting the flow to existing supply lines.

The intake port that is chosen to bring water into the pump is discretionary. Rear and front intakes require additional plumbing to be fabricated between the pump and the front bumper or rear of the body. The potential for friction loss, before the water

A 1994 E-One Sentry pumper with full stainless grille accents and a hydraulic ladder rack backed down the driveway for access to this house fire. The supply line was dropped by the second-due engine and brought to the side intake of Engine 44. The small square device on the cab roof between the emergency lights is a signaling device to control the traffic lights while the unit is responding.

The chauffeur is responsible for every item that is assigned to the pumper. After the fire, he or she will make sure that everything is returned to the appropriate place. This includes hose, tools, SCBA bottles, flashlights, radios, batteries, and fittings. Before leaving the scene, the chauffeur will make sure that all of the compartments are closed and the water tank is full.

Some departments order chauffeurs to remain with the rig (as opposed to being part of the engine company), and don't issue them full turn-out gear. The gear is expensive and is not needed unless the firefighter is going to enter a burning building. Other departments will assign the chauffeur as part of the attack company when the vehicle will not be used.

Fighting fires is the heart of engine work. Firefighters will use attack lines of varying sizes to handle different fire loads. A small one-room fire will be fought with a 1 1/2- or 1 3/4-inch line, while a heavier fire will necessitate a 2 1/2-inch line right from the start. Several attack lines on each pumper are preconnected to the fire pump and are ready to use as soon as they are removed from the engine. These are referred to as pre-connects or cross-lays depending on their location. The balance of the attack line on the rig is supplemental and used to lengthen the preconnects, or as additional attack lines.

reaches the pump, is the reason that some departments prefer to use the intakes that are integral to the pump itself. This provides the most direct path into the pump. Bearing in mind that many pumpers only have the intakes that are part of the pump, other concerns factor into the choice of which intake to use.

One example comes from the Los Angeles City Fire Department. The department specifies that all pumpers purchased have front and rear intake ports. This can be particularly important during the extensive brush fires that occur in that region. When a pumper uses the side intake directly into the pump, the hose line has to venture into the street before making a wide turn at the pump. When operating on narrow streets, this can hamper the arrival and deployment of additional fire rigs and make it more difficult for the civilians who are instructed to evacuate the neighborhood. By using a rear intake for a forward lay or a front intake with a reverse lay, the hose line remains in the same lane as the pumper, keeping passing lanes open.

When the first engine company arrives on the scene, the officer, who is in charge of the engine company, begins a size-up to determine what is happening. In order to size up the situation, he or she hopes to have a quick initial view of three sides of the structure. This includes the side of the building as they approach, the front of the building, and the far side as they pull slightly past leaving room for the aerial truck. At this point, only the rear of the structure has not had a cursory inspection, which will occur after preliminary jobs have begun.

Assuming there is a fire, the next step is to determine what is needed to attack this fire. The firefighters need to estimate how

The Chicago Fire Department purchased pumpers for years featuring Ford C Series cabs and chassis. Here, a firefighter calls for water to put his rig-mounted master stream to work. The large-diameter supply line has been laid but not yet charged.

Apparatus placement is important for both access and safety. This cab-forward pumper was parked too close to the fire. It suffered a cracked windshield along with melted turn signal and warning light domes from the intense heat.

After a firefighter arrives on the scene of a fire, he prepares his SCBA before leaving the jump seat area of the American LaFrance Pioneer pumper.

much hose is needed to reach the fire, what diameter attack line will be used, and which nozzle. A rule of thumb for the length of hose needed at the front door is to figure 50 feet per floor plus the depth of the building. Determining the diameter of attack line needed is often based on experience. Since a fire can double in size every minute, it may be necessary to look a little ahead. Otherwise, it's simple: a small fire means a small line and a big fire requires a big line. The next decision regards which nozzle to use. Basically, there are two types: a fog nozzle and a smooth-bore tip (also called a pipe). A smooth-bore nozzle has less pressure at the tip, which is easier on the firefighters. This can be advantageous for departments with less manpower. The smooth-bore nozzle also provides deeper penetration and superior reach, as compared to a fog nozzle that is set to release a straight stream with the same pressure.

The number one priority at a fire scene is to put water between the fire and the occupants, allowing for escape and rescue. Once the engine company is in place, it is necessary to cool the highest and hottest point of the fire to prevent inversion, or flashover. Even though each company's work is specific in its tasks, the bottom line at every working fire is that each task supports the nozzle man to get at the seat of the fire. When the structure has more than one floor, operations inside the building center around keeping control of or holding the stairways with a handline to aid in rescues and evacuations.

The primary function of the engine company has always been to extinguish fires. Although this is still the case today, an engine company's duties also include responding to motor vehicle accidents, rescues, and any emergency that prompts someone to dial 911. In recent years, another responsibility has been added, which in many cases has become the primary duty for some engine companies. Under the heading of EMS, engine companies have become first responders to assist with the growing number of emergency medical requests. Dispatched in addition to an ambulance or medic unit, the engine company assists with manpower or begins medical treatment if it arrives first. Since the number of fires nationally has declined in the past decade, firefighters are trained to handle medical calls with basic first aid training, Emergency Medical Technician (EMT) training, or as full paramedics, in addition to their training in firefighting.

A certain amount of medical supplies is also part of the equipment complement on each pumper. Depending on the level of trained personnel on board, pumpers may be stocked with basic life support (BLS) or advanced life support (ALS) equipment. As a matter of fact, an ALS-equipped pumper has all the capabilities of an ALS ambulance, except the means to transport a patient. Drugs, telemetry, and a defibrillator are part of an ALS engine, which is staffed by paramedics.

There are pumper designs that also incorporate patient-transport capabilities. As budgets shrink and medical responses increase, fire departments are looking for any means possible to combine duties and continue providing the highest-quality service to the public. In many cases, this is achieved by designing apparatus differently than in years past, and by equipping pumpers with the supplies necessary to help victims and patients.

When fire departments began providing EMS, an engine would be dispatched with an ambulance to provide additional manpower. Here, the crew of this 1969 Seagrave conventional B Series pumper is assisting medics after a head-on car collision.

CHAPTER 5
The Manufacturers of Today

The Custom Chassis Makers
HME

When Grumman Emergency Products closed its doors, HME released the 1871 Series chassis with tilt-cabs to the full fire service. Initially, there was one model offered that was available in several configurations. These cabs were constructed of 3/16-inch aluminum. The styles included the ER (stubby), SFDR (short four-door with a 10-inch raised roof), MFD (medium four-door), MFDR (medium four-door with a 10-inch raised roof), LFD (long four-door), LFDR (long four-door with a 10-inch raised roof), and the LFDSC (long four-door with a raised roof to any custom height).

In addition to the 1871 Series, HME offered the Classic Series, a low-profile fixed-cab design that had been used for the Grumman AerialCat. It featured the lowest profile cab in the industry, with just 88 inches from the ground to the top of the cab. The available configurations included the open jump seat version, which had a 9-inch raised roof over each rear-facing seat. The raised roof did not extend the entire width of the cab; instead it was notched in the center to accommodate an aerial device. The only other style that was offered had the same raised/notched roof but was fully enclosed with full-length LFD doors.

Smeal built four 1000-gpm pumpers in 1998 for Yonkers, New York. Each has an HME 1871 Series MFD cab and low-side compartments on the driver's side.

This is a 1998 custom top-mount, 1500-gpm pumper from Alexis. It features an HME 1871-P MFDR cab and chassis. The grille on the 1871-P Series is flat, whereas the 1871 Series has a grille that is over an inch thick.

Similar to other companies, the standard HME 1871 series features a rear door that is notched over the wheel well. There are custom HME chassis on the road, though, that do not conform to these standard designations. They were built to the unique specifications of the purchasing fire department and include longer extensions or different doors.

The Stubby is HME's terminology for a small cab that has only two doors and does not extend behind the front axle.

In an effort to simplify ordering a custom chassis, HME offers just one base model, which can incorporate all of the available engines, interior options, and trim packages. The SFD version comes standard with a 10-inch raised roof over the crew seating area. HME also introduced what it calls a "High Altitude" seating arrangement for the SFD. This raises the rear seats on a base platform that has storage compartments. In addition to the added storage, the benefits include raising the firefighters up to allow for easy egress with SCBAs on their backs. The MFD has seating for six and shares all of the components of the SFD and the LFD. The LFD can be configured to seat as many as 10 people with SCBA packs stored in each seat back. The MFD and LFD are available with flat roofs or 10- or 24-inch sloped, raised roofs. The rear door for the cabs

with a 10-inch raised roof is the same door that is used for cabs with flat roofs. The rear doors for cabs with the 24-inch roof extension are taller, full-height doors.

Between 1993 and 1996, HME produced a private label 1871 Series called the Intruder for the Ferrara Company. This allowed Ferrara to offer a single service warranty to customers that did not want to worry about a split responsibility between the chassis and body builders in the event of a service issue. The cabs offered a 3/16-inch-thick aluminum outer skin throughout the line with FFA-SFD, FFA FLD-MFD, FFA-LFD, and command cab model configurations corresponding to the Intruder Series. As with the 1871 Series, all of the rear doors were notched. The LFD was an extended MFD, and the command cab added a 24-inch roof extension to the LFD.

HME also offers a custom conventional chassis that was previously offered under the Hendrickson name. The HME VT-Fire is similar to the VT-100 conventional chassis that is offered for specialty trucks in other fields requiring a heavy-duty truck chassis. The VT-Fire is standard with either a two-door conventional cab or a four-door crew cab and can accommodate engines with up to 500 horsepower.

In 1994, HME introduced a full-height door for the cabs with a 10-inch raised roof and standardized this door for the cabs with a 24-inch raised roof also. The taller door that had been offered previously for these cabs could be special ordered as an option from this point forward. HME also offered its customers the option of special-order custom raised roofs. These could be designed with or without windows, although a 15-inch extension was the minimum to accommodate the installation of glass.

HME added the 1871-P Series to the product offerings in the same year. The P stood for Penetrator. This introduction brought a more economical chassis into the line that shared many of the 1871 Series options with a more conservative trim package. The use of smaller, more compact engines allowed for a lower doghouse. Cab configurations for the 1871-P Series were limited to the MFD and MFDR.

The 1871 SFO Series was also introduced in 1994. SFO is an abbreviation for short front overhang. This unit features a shortened cab length that was achieved by removing 28 inches of dead space between the front and rear seating areas. This shorter cab provides for a greater approach angle than any other custom chassis with a 45-degree steering cramp angle, giving an extremely tight turning radius. An additional feature includes a height of less than 13 feet when the cab is tilted. This allows for engine maintenance in many of the older firehouses around the country with lower ceilings. Another selling point for easy maintenance is HME's "wide-mouth doghouse" engine enclosure. It is a large cover next to the driver that opens easily and is held in place with a gas-charged strut. The SFO is constructed of galvanneal steel with aluminum doors.

HME engaged in a marketing program with the Smeal Fire Apparatus Company to provide the SFO chassis for a pumper program called the Watchdog. Designed for fire departments on tight budgets, the Watchdog program offered a full pumper package with minimal options.

Spencer, another small company building fire trucks, made this top-mount rescue pumper for the Gobles Pine Grove Fire Department in Michigan. It features an HME 1871 SFDR custom chassis. Attached to the front intake port is a section of hard suction hose that is preconnected for quick drafting operations. The intake port is attached to a fitting that turns so the hard suction can swivel toward the water and drop right in.

Southboro, Massachusetts, purchased this 1250-gpm rescue pumper from Central States in 1997. It is built on an HME 1871 SFO Series four-wheel drive chassis with an SMFD cab. Engine 21 carries 750 gallons of water.

In terms of safety, the SFO boasts a short 5-foot distance from the front bumper to the point on the ground that is visible to the driver. This compares to a range of 13 to 26 feet for commercial trucks. The SFO comes standard with a Cummins 8.3-liter, 300-horsepower engine and an Allison MD-3060 electronic transmission. The 1871-SFO is available with only two cab configurations. The first is the standard SMFD design and this is supplemented with a 10-inch raised roof SMFDR option. Seating in the SFO can be configured for a maximum of six firefighters.

To compare size, the SFO is over two feet shorter than an 1871 MFD. The distance is split between the length of the cab at the rear and the amount of the cab that extends in front of the axle. Compared to a commercial cab that is mass-produced and available to any truck purchaser, the SFO is almost six feet shorter.

After the introduction of the SFO, HME incorporated the 45-degree cramp angle into the entire 1871 Series of chassis, making these the most maneuverable vehicles in their respective classes.

In 1997, HME introduced the 1871-P2 Series. This was to be the entry-level model with a more modest trim package than the

1871-P. The 1871-P2 had a 1/8-inch aluminum shell, single headlights, side grills that were punched directly into the cab with no stainless cover, and no side crew windows. Like the 1871-P, the P2 had a lower doghouse than the 1871 Series since it was only available with the smaller engines.

The standard engine now for the SFO and 1871-P2 Series is the Cummins ISC with 300-horsepower. Upgrades include the 330 and 350-horsepower ISC engines, as well as the Detroit Series 40 with 300 or 330-horsepower. The standard transmission is the Allison MD-3060.

The release of the SFO-Lite Series was also in 1997. This model is available exclusively with the Cummins 275-horsepower ISB engine and the Allison MD-3060 transmission. This is designed primarily for rescue operations and units with a rear pump. The SFO-Lite has a lighter frame and suspension, along with smaller tires, while the cramp angle is increased to 48 degrees. If the unit is built with a rear pump and rear pump panel, the body can be shorter and still provide more space for storage than a conventional series pumper provides with a midship pump and panel. The SFO-Lite has a GVW of 31,000 pounds, compared with 36,600 pounds for the SFO.

As of 1999, the available roof configurations are as follows. Flat, a 12-inch raised roof with no windows, and a 24-inch raised roof with a variety of window options. The rear cab door is shared by the 12-inch and 24-inch versions, although a taller door for the 24-inch model is a custom option. The Classic for 1999 offers a full tilt-cab model with no grille but the same clean face as the previous fixed-cab. Classic engine options include the Detroit Series 60 and the Cummins M-11.

Other changes in 1999 include various features of the cab shells that were standardized between the 1871 Series, the 1871-P and P2 models. In terms of fabrication, the SFO cab beginning in 1999 has an all-aluminum shell with 1/8-inch sides to the cab and 3/16-inch doors. The P2 is completely 3/16-inch aluminum and offers a stainless-steel grille, quad headlights with turn signals, and a window for the jump seat position as standard. The 1871 Series and the 1871-P are also built completely of 3/16-inch aluminum. Galvanneal steel and stainless steel are available on a special-order basis. The engines available for the 1871-P Series include the Cummins 320-horsepower M-11 with options for the Cummins ISC and the new Detroit Series 40. The 1871

In 1994, 3D built twin pumpers for Haverhill, Massachusetts. They have high-side compartments, a top-mount pump panel, 1250-gpm pumps, and 500-gallon water tanks. The chassis are HME 1871-P Series with SFDR cabs.

Series offers the same engines, although options go up to the 500-horsepower Cummins M-11; the Cummins N14, ranging from 410 to 500 horsepower; the Detroit Series 60, ranging from 350 to 500 horsepower and the Caterpillar 3406, with 400-plus horsepower. Transmissions from Allison or Fuller Ceemat are available across the entire line.

Other changes for the SFO include additional cab configurations. A lengthened model incorporates a 9-inch rear extension that comes standard with a 12-inch raised roof. This would equate to a LSMFDR configuration, since the rear door is notched for the wheel well and has a smaller step than the 1871 Series. The flat roof SFO does not offer the 9-inch lengthening.

The first customer for the new SFO cabs is the Chicago Fire Department (CFD). The CFD is outfitting its three squads with two-piece companies. One unit has a Snorkel aerial device, while the chaser unit has a conventional squad-type body with many compartments. To date, there are 28 HME chassis in service with the City of Chicago, HME's largest customer.

HME considers itself perhaps the most versatile company that builds custom cabs and chassis configurations. Approximately 50 percent of the units it produces annually are one-of-a-kind designs based on customer requests.

Spartan

In 1990, Spartan expanded its product line and changed the model designations again. Six different models were now available with 16 cab configuration options. Spartan claimed to have the largest selection of fire truck chassis in the world. The models were the Diamond, Monarch, Charger, Gladiator, Baron, and the Silent Knight. Each appeared to share the same base contoured cab with the curved windshield. All but the Monarch conformed to Spartan's Series 90 with the Eurospace cabs. Letter designations were now in use to describe the size, shape, and door configurations available for each model. Most of the rear doors for extended cabs were notched to go around the wheel well, with the exception of the Monarch. The following describe the codes:

- SFD (short four-door)—Six-person cab with two side doors and two doors facing the rear that enclosed the jump seats.
- MFD (medium four-door)—Six-person, four side doors; the cab ends right behind the rear door, and there is a small side window between the two side doors.

- LFD (long four-door)—Ten-person, four side doors; the cab has an extension of approximately 1 foot beyond the rear door and the rear doors are notched around the wheel wells. (It should be noted that prior to this time, Spartan used the LFD designation to indicate full-length rear doors. Most other cab manufacturers designate an LFD to mean a full-length door, while an MFD curves over the wheel well.)
- LFDSC (long four-door super command)—Ten-person, four side doors; the same extension as the LFD with the addition of a 20-inch raised roof with windows and full-height rear doors.

The Diamond was the entry-level cab-over model, with the engine ahead of the front axle. It offered engines with 250 and 300 horsepower. Cab options included the SFD in galvanneal or stainless steel and MFD in galvanneal steel. The headlights were in a double housing and there was a small, flat, square grille in the face of the cab.

The Monarch was a cab-forward design that mounted the engine behind the front axle. It was a fixed-cab model that still offered a two-door model with open jump seats and seating for six. There was also an eight-person fully enclosed cab that was a true LFD with full-length rear doors. These cabs were offered in galvanneal steel, stainless steel, or aluminum. The engine options ranged from 300 to 450 horsepower, and there were side grilles but no front grille. All of the cab styles from this point in the line offered quad headlight housings.

The Charger was a full tilt-cab model of the cab-forward design that was available in an SFD or MFD configuration. Offering the same engines as the Monarch, the Charger could only be distinguished from the Monarch by the lack of side grills and the Series 90 design that brought the door and side windows level with the bottom of the front windshield. This could be ordered in galvanneal steel, stainless steel, or aluminum.

The top-of-the-line model, with the engine ahead of the front axle, remained the Gladiator Series. This line offered the full range of features and options, including engines with a horsepower range from 300 to 450. The expanded cab options included the SFD, MFD, LFD, and the LFDSC. Fabrication was strictly out of aluminum. The Gladiator continued to use a large, square grille that was over an inch thick.

The Baron offered a midmount engine design. The engine was placed behind the cab, which allowed for seating options for up to 12 people. This was a fixed- or tilt-cab style with MFD, LFD, and LFDSC cab configurations. The MFD and LFD cabs were aluminum, while the LFDSC was stainless steel. The engine range was from 300 to 450 horsepower.

Finally, Spartan rounded out its chassis line with the introduction of the Silent Knight. The name was derived from the lack of engine noise in the cab, since the engine was located behind the rear axle. The Silent Knight shared the same engine options as the Baron, as well as the same cab configurations and seating options to accommodate a maximum of 12 people.

In 1994, Spartan modified its product line slightly and standardized the model designations. There were still six models available now with more than 24 cab configurations. The models were the Metro Star, Diamond, Gladiator, Charger, Baron, and the Silent Knight. The fixed-cab Monarch was discontinued, and the Metro Star replaced the Diamond as the entry-level cab-over offering. All of the rear doors for extended cabs now were notched to go around the wheel well. Spartan added three cab configurations that are described by the following codes:
- ER (emergency rescue)—Two-person, two-door short cab.
- SMFD (short, medium four-door)—Six-person, four side doors. The rear door had a narrower step; the cab did not have a side window between the two doors but had a 10-inch raised roof with no windows in the raised portion.
- MFDSC (medium four-door super command)—Six-person, four side doors. The cab ended right behind the rear door; there were small side windows between the two side doors, with the addition of a 20-inch raised roof with windows.

WEST TUCKERTON

TOWNSHIP OF
LITTLE EGG HARBOR

WEST
TUCKERTON
FIRE COMPANY

7101
FIRE-RESCUE

7101

The West Tuckerton Fire Company in Little Egg Harbor Township, New Jersey, runs this rescue pumper that was built by Saulsbury in 1995. It features a stainless-steel body along with a Spartan XLMFDSC Gladiator cab and chassis with a roof extension that begins over the driver and officer for added headroom up front. The top-mounted operator's panel is located within the crew enclosure for the 1500-gpm pump.

The Metro Star was a tilt-cab model with the engine located ahead of the front axle. Engines ranged from 5.9 to 6.6 liters with 230 through 300 horsepower. This chassis was easily distinguished from the others by the smaller, more economical front grille that used to be offered with the Diamond, as well as the reduced trim package of chrome and lights. Cab options included the ER, SFD, SMFD, and MFD.

Next in line was the Diamond series. This too was a cab-over tilt-cab model with the engine ahead of the front axle. The Diamond offered larger engines with 250 to 320 horsepower. It offered the same cab options as the Metro Star but offered a more deluxe trim package.

The Gladiator remained as the top-of-the-line cab-over design with a full range of features and options including engines of 11 liters and up. The horsepower range was from 330 to 470, and the expanded cab options included the ER, SFD, SMFD, MFD, LFD, and the LFDSC.

Spartan still offered the cab-forward Charger series. The standard engines were the Detroit 6V92 or the 8V92, with available horsepower from 300 to 450. The only cab configurations offered were still the SFD and the MFD for a maximum of six persons.

The fixed-cab midmount Baron chassis was now offered in the SMFD configuration as well as the MFD, LFD, and LFDSC. The line was still rounded out with the rear-engine Silent Knight. The Silent Knight still shared the same engine options as the Baron, as well as the same seating options to accommodate a maximum of 12 people.

It could be extremely confusing to the casual observer trying to identify each of the Spartan models by sight. While the Metro Star, Diamond, and Gladiator featured different trim packages and some differences in the grille, Spartan offered their customers the option of upgrading the less-expensive models with trim packages matching the Gladiator. In essence, it could be virtually impossible to differentiate some of the finished models from the others. Spartan initiated a practice of placing a very small nameplate by the running light on the front corner of the cab that would identify the underlying chassis. Unfortunately, some of these did not end up remaining on the finished units, either from being pulled off or inadvertently left off.

Spartan includes a manufacturing tag inside every cab providing different types of information. One item is a coded model number that gives a very thorough description of the unit. The table below describes most, but not all of the possible combinations (Table 1).

In 1995, Spartan removed the Diamond from the offerings but introduced another innovative cab and chassis style, which it named the GT One. Like the Diamond, the GT One was an economical chassis. It shared a design characteristic, though, with the Silent Knight. The GT One mounted the engine behind the rear axle. The 6.6-liter, 300-horsepower Caterpillar 3116 was the standard engine, paired with the Allison MD 3060 electronic transmission. The cab had only one configuration, with four doors and a 10-inch raised roof. It was the first raised roof allowing

additional headroom for the driver and officer. If a letter designation were to be assigned to the GT One cab, it would probably be LSMFDR. The cab had an extension behind the rear door. The total distance from the center of the front axle to the back of the cab was 54 inches, which matches the midaxle-to-rear distance of an SMFD plus the extension of an LFD.

The GT One offered some new features for the fire truck industry. Seating accommodations in this cab were for seven people,

This is a Spartan GT One chassis with a custom rescue body built by Darley in 1995 for the Pittsfield, Massachusetts, Fire Department.

TABLE 1

Cab Type	Cab Material	Number of Doors	Roof Style	Cab Style	Number of Axles	Engine Position	Number of Wheels	Driving Wheels
M—Monarch	S-Steel	2- 2-door	0-Flat	S-SFD	2- 2 axles	0-Back*	4- 4 wheels	2- 2 wheels
S-Silent Knight	C-Stainless Steel	4- 4 door	1- 10-inch Rise	M-MFD	3- 3 axles	1-Forward	6- 6 wheels	4- 4 wheels
G-Gladiator	A-Aluminum		2- 20-inch Rise	L-LFD		2-Rear**		6- 6 wheels
B-Baron	F-Fiberglass		3- T- Notch	T-SMFD		3-Middle***		
D-Diamond			4- 3-inch Notch	E-ER				
C-Charger			5- 14-inch Rise	A-Ambulance				
A-Ambulance			6- 5-inch Rise	0-Other				
L-Metro Star								
R-Low-profile Gladiator								
F-Crash Truck								
V-Advantage								
T- TR-1								
N- GT One								

*Behind the front axle
**Silent Knight, GT One
***Baron

GA41M-2142
(Sample model)
The last digits of the VIN represent the sales order number

Anaheim, California, is one of several southern California cities to order midengine Stealth pumpers from Saulsbury. This is a 1995 pumper on a Spartan MFD Baron chassis with a 1250-gpm rear-mounted pump. It carries 500 gallons of water, along with 10 gallons of foam in a tank. The electronically controlled pump panel is located within the rear compartment on the driver's side.

and for the first time everyone would face forward. The raised roof also extended to the front seat instead of beginning in the crew area. In addition, the cab had a flat floor throughout.

The GT One was designed to have the fire pump in the rear. Most fire trucks have to be in gear to use the pump. The rear-engine design allowed the pump to be driven directly from the crankshaft, which in turn meant the transmission could remain in neutral. This also allowed the pump to be operated while the truck was in motion for incidents such as wildland fires. This is called "pump and roll." The intakes and discharges were located at the rear of the pumper to allow the hose in the hose bed to be preconnected for quick activation. The operator's control panel was located in a nearby compartment on the side of the vehicle. Unlike the trend to widen cabs to create more room, the GT One was actually narrower than the rest of the line. The rear engine allowed the

cab, with an overall width of just 87 inches instead of the normal 94 inches, to offer as much interior room as other cabs.

One other feature designed into the GT One was smaller tires to lower the overall height. This eliminated wheel wells, providing a flat and level floor inside the cab. Also in 1995, the Charger, Baron, and Silent Knight models were capable of accepting larger engines with 470 horsepower.

The GT One proved to be a more difficult chassis for many body fabricators to build on, so these companies opted not to push the model heavily. Due to the lack of demand, Spartan discontinued the GT One in 1997 after producing roughly 30 of them.

Shortly after eliminating the GT One, Spartan introduced the Total Response One (TR-1). This new model features a full tilt-cab design available in an MFD configuration only. The TR-1 comes standard with a 275-horsepower Cummins ISB engine and the Allison MD-3060P six-speed automatic transmission. The cab interior has a flat floor, accommodates five firefighters with forward-facing seats, and features perhaps the lowest engine tunnel available today. The TR-1 is designed for rescue and medical applications for ambulances or combination units that also have a pump and carry water. The crew area is designed with an option for fold-up seats to allow for additional crew maneuverability. The cab configuration is an SMFD with a small, flat grille like the Metro Star. There is no window between the two doors, nor is there a grille on the side of the cab. Similar to the Metro Star, the headlights are mounted in a dual housing with turn signals mounted on the corners of the cab, although the quad lights are optional.

Currently, the Spartan line includes the Advantage, the Metro Star, the TR-1, and the Gladiator. The Advantage was introduced in 1996 and is the entry-level chassis series meant to compete with the mass-produced commercial chassis. The Cummins ISC Series with 300, 330, or 350-horsepower engine is used in this chassis. There is a choice of four different Allison automatic transmissions, with the standard model being the MD-3060P. The Advantage has an aluminum cab and includes antilock brakes (ABS), features a flat grille on the face of the cab, and comes standard without a window between the two doors on the side of the cab. The full tilt-cab has seating for six with an option for a 10-inch raised roof, making an MFDR configuration. The body builder, not Spartan, may add a side window to this cab for the customer. The Advantage also comes standard with rubber fenders, and the engine ventilation slots on the side of the cab are cut directly into the cab.

The next model in the line is the Metro Star. This is also a full tilt-cab design that offers the same Cummins ISC engines as the Advantage in addition to the ISM 380-horsepower engine. The MD-3060P transmission is also standard on the Metro Star as well as ABS. The available cab configurations include MFD, LFD, SMFD, and ER with 10-inch or 20-inch raised roof extensions and full-height doors. The Metro Star also has a flat, square grille that is in the center of the cab

face. When originally introduced, the Metro Star was the lowest model. When the Diamond was eliminated to reduce the confusion between the various cab-over entries, the Metro Star moved up a notch to make room for the Advantage.

The top-of-the-line model remains the full tilt-cab Gladiator. The standard engine currently is the Cummins 400-horsepower ISM engine, with an option to use the Detroit Diesel Series 60 engine. The Allison HD-4060P is standard as is ABS. Cab configurations available are the same as those offered for the Metro Star. The Gladiator retains the large, thick grille that has been a trademark for many years.

The Silent Knight, the Baron, and the Charger models are considered specialty items, and though they are not highly advertised, they can be requested on a special-order basis.

Spartan began to expand its presence in the fire apparatus industry with the acquisition of two companies that build fire truck bodies. Luverne and Quality became wholly owned subsidiaries of Spartan in 1997 and part of the new Emergency Vehicle Team. In 1998, Spartan further advanced its position with the acquisition of Road Rescue, a company that builds ambulances. Spartan added to its product line chassis that are tailored for the ambulance industry. In addition to building chassis for the fire industry, Spartan builds chassis for school buses, transit buses, step vans, and motorhomes.

Body Builders
3D, 4 Guys, Alexis, Central States, Ferrara

3D Fire Apparatus is located in Shawano, Wisconsin, and has been building fire trucks since the early 1970s. Until recently, its work was largely for other companies that labeled the units as their own, such as Pierce, Darley, Seagrave, and Grumman. Today, it builds from aluminum, galvanneal steel, and stainless steel. 3D does not use model names or model numbers. 3D is a builder of custom fire trucks using any chassis requested by their customers. 3D's largest customer is the City of San Francisco Fire Department, which has over 41 3D units. In 1998, the American LaFrance Division of the Freightliner Corporation purchased a controlling interest in 3D.

The Centurion Lite primary response vehicle from Central States Fire Apparatus is built on an HME SFO Lite SMFD chassis. Mounting the pump and electronic operator's controls at the rear of the unit allows more storage compartment space throughout the unit. The intake and discharge ports are also in the rear, which allows all of the compartments to be wider than on a conventional pumper.

4 Guys, Inc., is a manufacturer of stainless-steel pumpers, rescues, and elliptical tankers. Located in Meyersdale, Pennsylvania, since its founding in 1974, it builds on commercial and custom chassis from HME, Spartan, and American LaFrance. The 4 Guys company offers pumps from Hale, Waterous, and Darley and specializes in 90-day deliveries from the time they receive the chassis. Pumpers are available with side- or top-mounted control panels and custom body designs based on the customer's specifications.

Alexis Fire Equipment began building fire trucks in 1947 in the town of Alexis, Illinois. It builds pumpers, rescues, and aerial bodies for customers that are mainly located in the Midwest. It too is a custom builder and does not have model names and numbers specific to its products. Alexis builds on commercial and custom chassis.

Central States Fire Apparatus is located in Lyons, South Dakota. It manufactures custom pumper bodies, made of galvanneal steel, stainless steel, or aluminum, using commercial or custom chassis. During 1997, in cooperation with HME, Central introduced the

Centurion and Centurion Lite Series. They feature HME's 1871 SFO and SFO-Lite chassis respectively. The Centurion is a rescue pumper designed to assist departments that handle EMS, rescue, and hazmat (hazardous materials) duties, in addition to fires. It features roll-up doors and a side-mounted operator's panel, keeping the unit as compact as possible. The Centurion Lite is a primary response vehicle providing departments with a smaller unit that has a large amount of compartment storage. Its storage rivals that of much bigger units. The Centurion Lite has a rear-mounted pump, with the operator's panel, discharges, and intake ports also in the rear. Both units have tall and deep rescue-style compartments. Putting the operator's panel and piping at the pumper's rear shortens the body considerably and allows Central to widen the compartments to provide more space.

Ferrara Fire Apparatus (FFA) is located in Holden, Louisiana. It builds pumpers, rescues, and aerial fire apparatus bodies. FFA offers two different styles of bodies. The first features bodies constructed of

extruded aluminum, while the second offers modular bodies of aluminum, galvanneal steel, or stainless steel. It offers side- or top-mounted pump panels and many options for body layouts. Between 1993 and 1996, Ferrara offered the Intruder custom fire chassis, manufactured for them by HME, with SFD, MFD, and LMFD configurations. The SFD was available as an SFDR with a 10-inch raised roof and as an SFD SC with a 20-inch raised roof. The MFD and LMFD were offered with a 10-inch extension, as the LMFDR and MFDR.

Ferrara has what it refers to as program trucks. These are full pumpers with limited options that can be built in a short time for a low price. One of these models is the Interceptor, which features a custom HME 1871-P MFDR chassis with no side window. Previously, the Interceptor featured a Spartan Advantage MFD chassis, also with no side window. Both Interceptors have a 300-horsepower Cummins C8.3 engine, 1250-gpm pump, 750-gallon tank, galvanneal steel body, and a small list of available

options, to offer a price point of under $150,000. The other program pumper is a commercial pumper featuring a Freightliner FL-80 chassis with a two-door cab and features similar to the Interceptor, but with a price of $104,800.

In 1998, at the International Association of Fire Chiefs Convention in Louisville, Ferrara introduced its own custom chassis series called the Inferno. The cab is extruded aluminum with 3/16-inch outer panels. FFA designed a new steering system from the column to the axle that is exclusive to the Inferno. As an ergonomic improvement, FFA includes 11 control switches in the steering wheel for ease of access for the driver. The cab has a contoured design with a bright chrome grille and a large grid pattern that matches the quad headlight housings on either side. The cab configuration is an MFDR with a full-height door and a 10-inch raised roof that begins midway over the driver's door, extending to the rear wall. The seating accommodates six firefighters. The standard engine is the Detroit Diesel 500-horsepower

This pumper for Cockeysville, in Baltimore County, Maryland, was built by 4 Guys. It features a Freightliner FLD 120 chassis with a four-door crew conversion. It was built in 1992 with a 1500-gpm pump and a 1,000-gallon water tank.

In an attempt to lower the cost of apparatus, the Baltimore County Fire Department purchased seven pumpers from Luverne in 1994 using Freightliner FL-80 four-door crew-cab chassis with roof extensions. The pumpers were identical except for the name of the station painted on the rear door. Each has a trash line (a 25 foot preconnected hose) stored on the front bumper in a custom-built box.

Series 60, paired with an Allison MD4060P five-speed automatic transmission. The first 100 Infernos will have an engraved plate which is signed by the owner and numbered sequentially.

Luverne

Luverne Fire Apparatus has been building fire trucks since 1912. It was a regional builder in Luverne, Minnesota, for many years, selling few trucks in other areas of the country. In 1985, Luverne Fire Apparatus was purchased by Luverne Truck Equipment and moved to South Dakota, where it began an aggressive campaign to compete nationally. In the early 1990s, Luverne burst onto the national scene after securing a large pumper contract with the Chicago Fire Department. The first order was for 23 units, which increased to a total of 38 in just a few years. These units were built on Spartan MFD Diamond chassis. Luverne went on to build two specialty units on commercial chassis for the Chicago air mask unit. In 1996, Chicago changed to the new HME SFO chassis and ordered eight more pumpers from Luverne.

In 1998, there were 10 additional units with the HME chassis for a total of 56 Luverne pumpers by the beginning of 1999.

Luverne is a custom builder that has made many pumpers with unique configurations and custom crew enclosures. One such order was for a pair of pumpers going to Great Falls, Montana. The department ordered two units built on Freightliner cab-over chassis with a special crew compartment between the cab and body. The enclosure also houses the pump operator's station, to provide a controlled environment to offset the severe winter temperatures that occur in Montana.

Luverne also secured an order with the Baltimore County Fire Department for seven pumpers utilizing the Freightliner Business Class chassis with a four-door cab and a raised roof. A strong dealer network has made Luverne a formidable player in the national pumper market.

For many years, Luverne offered the Commando/Commander line of custom pumpers. Commander Models I through IV were custom pumpers with formed bodies fabricated from aluminum, stainless steel, or galvanneal steel. The designations indicated the size of the body and the maximum water tank capacity that corresponded to each size. The Commando offered a 20 1/2-inch compartment between the pump and the rear wheel. The Commander I had a 32-inch compartment, Commander II a 36-inch, Commander III a 51 1/2-inch compartment, and the Commander IV had a 57-inch rescue-style compartment. The standard compartment behind the rear wheel for all of these models was 36 inches wide. If a fire department wanted to substitute a 51 1/2-inch rear compartment with any of the standard front compartments, then the model would belong in the XL Series and the name would gain the XL suffix. Thus, a pumper with a 36-inch compartment in front of the rear wheel and a 51 1/2-inch compartment behind the rear wheel would be a Commander II XL. The maximum water tanks corresponding to each model in order was 750, 1,000, 1,250, 1,500, and 1,800 gallons, respectively.

Luverne builds custom pumpers on both HME and Spartan chassis. For several years, many of Luverne's dealers favored the HME chassis over the Spartan. This changed in 1997, when Spartan purchased Luverne and also Quality, another fire apparatus body builder.

In early 1993, Luverne introduced the Legend Series of pumpers. This was the top-of-the-line model and offered a formed body in steel or aluminum. For simplicity, the Legend series carried model numbers that represented the length of the body. For example, a pumper with a body that was 152 inches was called a Legend 1520.

The next introduction was the Tradition Series, which offered tubular stainless-steel bodies. In 1998, Luverne introduced the TSS line of pumpers. The TSS body of tubular stainless steel replaced the Tradition. Custom and commercial pumpers are offered with side- or top-mounted pump panels and the choice of an EX model on a stock chassis with standard options, or an LX model with unlimited options.

Also in 1998, the Lear series was introduced, featuring an all-extruded aluminum body. Lear stands for Luverne Extruded Aluminum Revolution and represents one of the first extruded aluminum bodies designed exclusively in-house. Like the TSS, the Lear has EX and LX models with the same options and restrictions.

Since its purchase by Spartan, which also owns Quality, Luverne's product line was modified. The dealer networks of both companies were combined, so Luverne now offers aluminum extruded bodies and tubular stainless-steel bodies, while Quality offers formed bodies of both galvanneal and stainless steel.

Quality

Quality entered into the fire service in 1962 as a company that refurbished equipment for the U.S. government, primarily airport fire fighting crash trucks. It expanded into the production of new fire apparatus in the early 1980s and was purchased by Union City Body Corp. in the mid-1980s. It divested the refurbishing business in 1990 in order to focus all of its attention on the market for new fire trucks. In 1992, Quality was purchased by a group of its officers. Five years later, Spartan Motors purchased Quality. Quality builds commercial and custom pumpers as well as aerial apparatus bodies.

Today, as part of the Emergency Vehicle Team, Quality offers apparatus that is constructed from galvanneal or stainless steel, while its new sister company, Luverne, fabricates from aluminum and stainless steel.

Quality offers the Avenger rescue pumper series, which is a budget line with limited features and options. The Avenger is galvanneal steel and can be built on a commercial or custom chassis. The standard pump is a Hale 1500-gpm that is paired to a 750-gallon booster tank. The commercial model uses a Freightliner FL-80 two- or four-door cab and chassis. The custom model has a Spartan Advantage chassis, an MFD cab, and a Cummins ISC 300-horsepower engine. The options include a top-mounted pump panel, 330-horsepower engine, 1250-gpm pump, and a 1,000-gallon water tank.

Quality also has the Americana pumper series. This is a step-up model featuring a Spartan Metro Star chassis with an MFDR cab that includes a 10-inch raised roof. The engine is the Cummins 360-horsepower M-11, and the pump is a Waterous 1750-gpm paired with a 750-gallon water tank. The body is fabricated out of 12-gauge, 304L stainless steel.

Saulsbury

The Saulsbury Company has been building fire trucks for many years. Known principally for its custom specialized rescue units, it also builds pumpers. Offering a complete line that includes custom and commercial chassis, the majority of the Saulsbury pumpers feature Spartan, Duplex, and HME chassis. Many of its pumpers are in fact pumper-rescues that incorporate traditional characteristics of a pumper plus several attributes of a rescue squad. This enables a more versatile vehicle to provide additional capabilities at the scene of an emergency. A pumper-rescue features supplemental lighting, a generator, and large-capacity storage compartments for the required rescue and extrication equipment. The shape and configurations of rescue compartments differ from those on a standard pumper. Built like a heavy rescue, Saulsbury pioneered the use of removable equipment boxes, shelves that roll out and down to access equipment, and roller-bearing, slide-out tool boards as part of a pumper.

Another Saulsbury specialty is a "Diagrammatic" pump panel. Instead of merely listing the location of each discharge on the pumper, Saulsbury adds a diagram of the unit to the operator's control panel with arrows depicting the discharge corresponding to each gauge. Saulsbury pumpers are fabricated from galvanneal steel, stainless steel, formed aluminum, or extruded aluminum, though it is known principally for building with stainless steel. The finished Saulsbury bodies are always beautiful.

In 1994, Saulsbury introduced the Stealth Pumper Series. These pumpers were offered on a Spartan or Duplex chassis with a midmount engine positioned behind the cab. Bodies were fabricated from stainless steel. The designs boasted a low profile with superior weight distribution and maneuverability. The engine placement meant that the cab area was roomier, quiet, and not as hot. Each pump was crankshaft driven, featured one of the diagrammatic pump panels, and had hydraulically activated pump valves. The pump could be positioned in the front or, as is most common, in the rear with capacities up to 3500 gpm and water tanks with capacities to 4,000 gallons.

Saulsbury also offers the J-Series pumpers. These are stainless-steel units with modular bodies. The pump can be located in the rear or midship mounted. Different models that are available include the J2i, the J3i, and the J4i. The J2i features a midship pump, while the J3i is a rear-mounted unit. The J4i is a rescue unit with no pump.

In 1998, Saulsbury was purchased by the Federal Signal Corporation and became part of the Fire Rescue Group along with E-One. This purchase served to increase E-One's product offerings with the addition of stainless steel and galvanneal steel as building materials. Custom Saulsbury pumpers now include the Cyclone, Hurricane, and Hush chassis.

Smeal

Smeal built its first fire truck in 1963 and has been building them ever since. It offers pumpers, rescue squads, and aerials on both commercial and custom chassis. In conjunction with HME, Smeal introduced the Watchdog Series. This was a short pumper with a 165-inch wheelbase and a

The fire department in Cherry Valley, Illinois, owns nothing but E-One apparatus. When Saulsbury became part of the Fire Rescue Group of Federal Signal like E-One, Cherry Valley had access through E-One to purchase a new AM General Hummer that is outfitted for off-road wildland fires. This 1999 unit has a remote-controlled bumper turret, and carries water and foam to handle any situation firefighters may encounter.

side-mounted pump panel, or a 180-inch wheelbase with a top-mounted operator's panel built on an HME SFO chassis. The Watchdog had a Cummins C8.3 325-horsepower engine with an Allison MD3060 transmission, a 1000-gpm pump, and a 750 gallon tank. Options include pumps from Waterous or Hale with capacities up to 1500 gpm, a water tank that can hold 1,000 gallons, and a body fabricated from aluminum.

Smeal offers a unibody construction that came from the automotive industry. The body is fabricated with 12-gauge galvanneal steel that is formed and welded together, which allows the pump to be mounted directly to the body instead of the chassis frame.

Complete Apparatus Builders
American LaFrance

In 1995, the Freightliner Corporation purchased all of the assets and name rights of the defunct American LaFrance Company (ALF). As a means of preserving the rich tradition that ALF had with the fire service, Freightliner vowed to revive the name, tradition, and sense of styling that were lost when the company closed its doors. In addition, the new American LaFrance would be at the forefront of applying technology to the fire service with the vast resources that Freightliner had to offer.

The name Freightliner has been strongly associated with the fire service since 1991, when it introduced the Business Class Series of commercial chassis. This was the first genuine competition to the market strength held by Navistar's 4900 Series commercial chassis. When Ford discontinued the popular C-8000 tilt-cab series, Navistar stepped up to fill the void with the two- and four-door 4900 Series. When the Business Class entered the market, many fire departments began to specify these models for pumpers, ambulances, rescues, and the occasional aerial.

The Business Class is available in six models. The FL-50, FL-60, FL-70, FL-80, FL-106, and the FL-112 are available with four-wheel drive options, two-door cabs,

In 1998, RD Murray became part of the Freightliner American LaFrance family supplying stainless-steel apparatus bodies. It built the body on this ALF-148 Eagle chassis with a raised roof for Emerson, New York.

A Pierce Responder commercial pumper features a Freightliner FL-80 Business Class chassis. The specs for this 1997 unit include a 1500-gpm pump and a 1,250-gallon water tank for the Stonersville Fire Company of Exeter Township, Pennsylvania.

extended cabs, and four-door enclosed crew cabs with or without raised roofs. Each successive model has a greater GVW ranging from the FL-50 with 18,000 to 22,000 pounds, to the FL-112 with 33,000 to 62,000 pounds. Engines range from a low of 160 to a maximum of 450 horsepower. The two-door cab seats two or three, the extended cab seats four to five, and the crew cab can seat up to six firefighters. In addition to general acceptance from the fire departments, the Business Class Series is popular with body builders, who promote these chassis heavily with their bodies. A look at the sales literature for any body builder shows samples that were built on Business Class chassis.

In addition to the medium-duty Business Class chassis, Freightliner also offers its Class 8, FLD 120 conventional chassis for the fire service. These big rigs make for some very interesting fire trucks.

When Freightliner purchased American LaFrance and announced the release of a custom fire truck chassis, many of the complete fire truck builders that make their own cus-

tom chassis had to consider their options. Feeling that Freightliner was now a competitor, several of these other companies began to shy away from the commercial Freightliner chassis in favor of the Navistar 4900 Series.

In 1996, amid quite a bit of fanfare, the new American LaFrance Eagle Series custom fire truck chassis was introduced at the International Fire Chiefs' Convention in Kansas City, Missouri. This new cab and chassis had a contoured cab that resembled the American LaFrance Century Series. Unlike the Century that flared out for the jump seat area, the Eagle cab was full width all the way back. It was first introduced with an MFD configuration with short, barrier clearance doors and an exposed step. It was a full tilt-cab design with grilles on each side of the cab over the wheel wells and a large stainless-steel grille on the front. The front grille was wider than it was high and had horizontal louvers. All of the forward-facing headlights, emergency lights, and turn signals were in a single housing with a stainless steel band that bordered it. Like the Century, the lower portion of the cab face jutted out slightly, with a ridge just below the windshield. A second version with a 10-inch raised-roof MFDR configuration was also introduced along with the MFD. The Eagle was introduced with a custom-designed emergency light-bar that covered the full cab width and curved back on each side. Within a year, several body builders had completed units using the Eagle chassis.

The Detroit Diesel Series 55 engine with 400 horsepower was standard with options for the Series 60 with up to 500 horsepower, the Cummins M11+, or the Caterpillar C-12 engine. The standard transmission was the Allison HD-4060P five-speed with electronic push-button controls.

American LaFrance also builds fire pumps that have always been standard on its apparatus. This is still the case with the new Eagle Series, with a 1500-gpm midship single-stage pump as standard, with options up to 2000 gpm. American LaFrance is the only chassis manufacturer to furnish its own factory-installed pumps. The aluminum cabs have 1/8-inch-thick outer walls and 1/4-inch-thick inner walls.

The Eagle Series utilizes the model numbers ALF-134 and ALF-148, based on the distance from the front of the cab to the rear of the cab. In addition to the MFD and MFDR configurations, other options include an LMFD and LMFDR. Cabs with a 10-inch raised roof have a full-height door with a one- or two-piece window.

The ALF-134 provides seating for four in the standard configuration, with a maximum capacity of six. The ALF-148 has seating for six and can accommodate up to eight firefighters. American LaFrance provides a feature called the Officer Information Center with each Eagle. This consists of a small dashboard console in front of the officer that displays the vehicle speed, a compass, an external thermometer, the current time, the time of their response, and their arrival time on the scene. The officer can also set an alarm to indicate if the driver exceeds a predetermined speed, as well as a seatbelt alarm that signals if a passenger is not wearing his or her seatbelt.

This American LaFrance Eagle Series ALF-134 chassis has a body by M&W, another regional apparatus builder. The New Midway Volunteer Fire Company Number 9 is in Maryland. This 1998 unit is classified as a pumper-tanker, since it carries 1,500 gallons of water.

This is a view of the rear wall of an E-One Sentry pumper cab. Standard seating is for six, with four in the crew area. Two face forward while two face the rear.

In 1998, American LaFrance introduced the Eagle chassis in a low-profile design with a 100-inch height from the ground to the top of the cab. This design is six inches lower than the standard Eagle cabs. Engine options include the Detroit Diesel Series 60, Caterpillar CFE, and the Cummins ISC. The low-profile cab is available in the same two lengths as the standard Eagle. The ALF-134L and the ALF-148L share all of the external and internal characteristics of the ALF-134 and the ALF-148. The low-profile cabs are intended mainly for use with aerial apparatus.

Also in 1998, Freightliner and American LaFrance purchased a controlling interest in several smaller, regional fire apparatus body builders as well as aerial device manufacturers. 3D in Wisconsin, RD Murray in New York, Ladder Towers, Inc. in Pennsylvania, and the Snorkel line of aerial products were incorporated into the American LaFrance family along with Aerial Innovations, which was acquired in 1997 to produce a full service, single source complete fire apparatus builder.

In 1999 at the Fire Department Instructor's Conference in Indianapolis, American LaFrance introduced the Metropolitan custom fire and emergency service chassis. This entry-level custom chassis is a step between the Business Class and the Eagle Series. Four configurations are available including the ALF-123 MFD, ALF-135 LMFD, the ALF-123R MFDR, and the ALF-135R LMFDR. Again, the model number depicts the length of the cab from the front to the rear wall,

and the raised-roof models have a 14-inch extension. The extruded aluminum cabs feature 1/8-inch walls and utilize the Caterpillar CFE 300-horsepower engine as standard, with the Allison MD-3060P automatic transmission. Like the Eagle Series, the Metropolitan features short, barrier-style doors. The side grilles, the front grille, and the quad headlight housings resemble the Eagle in design, although instead of stainless steel, they are formed from molded plastic. The Metropolitan has a shorter windshield and the cab front below the windshield line slopes like other cabs, without the curved ledge that is part of the Eagle cab.

Standard seating in the ALF-123 is for four firefighters with an option to add two more. The ALF-135 easily seats eight and can accommodate a maximum of ten. The Metropolitan is a full tilt-cab model.

E-ONE

By 1993, there was one commercial pumper model that was available from E-One, simply called the commercial pumper. Since the tilt-cab was gone, there was no longer a reason to specify the line as conventional. The customer could choose a chassis by Freightliner, Peterbilt, Navistar, Ford, GMC/White, or Volvo with two-door or four-door crew cab models. The bodies were available with standard designs or could be customized at the fire department's request. Side- and top-mounted pump panels were offered with Hale or Godiva pumps. Standard tank sizes had 500 to 1,000-gallon capacities.

The custom pumper line was divided into Protector Pumpers, Cyclone Pumpers, Hurricane Pumpers, and Hush Pumpers. The Protector line offered four basic cab configurations. The short cab (SMFD), the medium cab (MFD), the long cab (LFD), and the extra-long cab (XLFD). Each style was also available with a raised vista roof option from 12 to 20 inches in 2-inch increments. Unlike other builders, the E-One vista roof extension was set in slightly from the edge of the cab roof. It was mounted on top of the cab above the rain gutter and had one long window on the side instead of two windows. The vista

portion was mounted in this manner so that it did not compromise the integrity of the cab extrusions.

These full tilt-cab pumpers had a low doghouse that gave a large opening between the crew and front areas of the cab. The Protector still had the same large square stainless-steel grille on the face of the cab, the small side grilles, and was available with a variety of trim options to dress up the appearance. The available engines ranged from 250 to 300 horsepower with an Allison MD 3060 five-speed transmission. Hale or Godiva pumps were offered along with water tanks from 500 to 1,000 gallons.

The Cyclone was still available as a fixed- or tilt-cab version. The fixed-cab had no front grille, but it had a vertical grille on the side. The tilt-cab had the large front grille and small side grilles like the Protector. Both styles offered 7 inches more interior height than the fixed-cab Hurricane. All three models offered Detroit or Cummins engines, and the Allison HT-740 four-speed transmission was standard. Water tanks in sizes of 500 to 2,500 gallons were offered, though the largest required a tandem rear axle. The Hurricane was a lower

profile design and the cab configurations were MFD and LFD. The Cyclone had the MFD and LFD, while the Cyclone TC was available as an SMFD, MFD, LFD, or XLFD. Again, the vista roof options were offered in several heights.

The Hush Pumper offered 500, 750, or 1,000-gallon water tanks with a selection of Hale pumps. Detroit Diesel or Cummins rear-mounted engines were again available and the Hush had an optional sliding access panel on the side of the pumper for engine access. The rear compartments slid back to provide walk-up access on either side of the engine. Cab seating would accommodate up to 10 firefighters, and the unique Hush design made the seating layouts flexible to meet the needs of each department. Exterior cab configurations were the same as those offered for the Cyclone TC, except that there were no grilles at all in the cab.

E-One introduced a new chassis in 1993 called the Sentry. This was a lower cost, engine-forward, full tilt-cab with limited options. It featured a 44-degree cramp angle and was available in an MFD configuration only, with a maximum seating capacity of eight. The Sentry was designed for the Cummins 6CTA engine with 250 to 300

The Chemical Hook and Ladder Company of Colonia, New Jersey, owns an E-One LFD Hush rescue pumper. The fire company ordered the cab without a jump seat window to maximize the storage space. The top-mount unit has rescue-style compartments with roll-up doors and a roof-mounted telescoping light tower to illuminate any scene at night. The rear rescue compartment has slide-out shelving for quick access to the hydraulic rescue tools.

horsepower, along with the Allison MD 3060 five-speed transmission. This was the first E-One unit that offered a choice of Hale or Waterous pumps. Water tanks with 500- to 1,250-gallon capacities were offered as well as a choice of side or top-mounted controls. Standard air vents for the front and side of the Sentry cab were cut directly into the cab surface and painted to match. The same style front stainless-steel grille that the Protector and Cyclone TC models used was an option to dress up the cab, along with a stainless-steel side grille over the front axle.

With the exception of the Sentry, all of E-One's custom cabs have lap-style front doors that are not flush with the body and feature an outer panel that is curved over the wheel well. The cutout for the door itself is not curved; instead it is angled to a point where it goes straight down to meet the step. The same is true for the rear MFD doors and openings. As a cost saving for the Sentry, the doors do not have the outer, overlapping, contoured skin. They are flush with the side of the cab and have straight lines around the wheel well instead of the curved design. As with other models, the Sentry can be dressed up with different trim packages.

E-One was also marketing a complete line of industrial pumpers that featured commercial or custom chassis. Some of the op-

tions for these units included high-capacity dual agent delivery, foam systems, high-volume pumps with up to 3000-gpm capacities, along with high-volume deck guns to deliver the foam and water. Foam capacity ranged from 500 to 3,000 gallons of 3M Light Water ATC foam concentrate.

In 1994, E-One was marketing a new Hush EMS Series. This model provided space and access for patient treatment and transport in the rear portion of the cab. The standard configuration was a modified three-door MFD cab with a 10-inch raised roof that had no windows. The slightly wider-than-normal rear door was on the passenger side of the cab, while the driver's side was solid from the front door to the rear of the cab. The window over the wheel well on this side was replaced with a pass-through storage compartment giving additional access to equipment and supplies. The cab had seating for four, with one seat near the gurney, allowing a medic to tend to a patient. The raised roof incorporated overhead storage for EMS supplies, and the patient treatment area had a built-in oxygen system. The cab could also be configured as an XLFD to provide even greater room for patient treatment.

This unit had a rear-mounted 1500-gpm pump with a fully enclosed pump

The majority of the fleet for the O.W.L. Fire Company in Woodbridge, Virginia, is from E-One. This 1997 pumper features a Hurricane TC LMFDR cab and chassis with a full-height rear door, a 1500-gpm pump, 620-gallon water tank, and a 40-gallon foam tank. The horizontal piece that is supported over the rear of the hose bed is a directional arrow stick lightbar.

panel that was positioned at the rear of the unit on the curbside. All of the compartments had roll-up style doors with an option for standard lap doors. The actual pump panel was smaller than most because the discharge and suction connections were at the vehicle's rear.

The Hurricane, with its lower overall height, was introduced as a tilt-cab in 1994. This midengine design still offered a bench seat in the front that could seat three firefighters, although the most popular layout accommodated only the driver and the officer. The rear had seating for four, making this a six, or possibly a seven-seat cab. The Hurricane tilt-cab also offered raised roof options with full-height doors in the MFD and LFD configurations. The only way to discern a fixed Hurricane from a tilt-cab is to examine the space between the front of the cab face and the diamond plate deck on the front bumper. The fixed-cab will have a narrower space.

In 1995, E-One extended the Sentry options by offering a raised roof. Also in 1995, E-One announced the American Eagle product line. This offered pre-engineered apparatus with limited options that could be ordered on a commercial or custom chassis. This line was initially intended to focus on the rural fire market. The complete line consisted of pumpers, tankers, and rescue units. The name was borrowed from a smaller apparatus company formed by a group of former E-One employees that was later purchased by E-One in 1992.

E-One made several major changes in the chassis lineup in 1996. The Protector Series, the Sentry Series, and the Cyclone fixed-cab series were discontinued. These changes were preempted by the introduction of the new Cyclone II. With this new series, E-One increased the cab configuration options by making full-height doors available for models that featured a raised roof. Although the older vista roof was still available, the newer style became very popular. All of the cab configurations were still offered with seating for 6 to 10 firefighters depending on the design.

The Cyclone II maintained the familiar front grille but no longer used the external side grilles. Instead, the side vents were

changed to channel air into the wheel wells. This chassis offered a 45-degree steering cramp angle. The interior featured a redesigned doghouse that allowed for more room in the cab. Designed around the new in-line six-cylinder drivetrains, both medium- and heavy-duty engines could be accommodated with the same, smaller engine enclosure. The Cyclone II had improved dashboard ergonomics and maximized the seating space for the driver and officer. Since E-One had full-height doors, the vista roof options were now limited to 12-, 16-, or 20-inch heights. The available cab configurations were SMFD (44 inches from the axle to the rear wall), MFD (58 inches), LFD (67 inches), and LMFD (80 inches).

In 1998, the American Eagle Series featured a range of products offered with specific features, special pricing, and financing. Commercial pumpers started at $99,000 on a Ford F-800 chassis and ranged to $137,000 on an IHC 4900 chassis with a crew cab. A new chassis offering E-One called a super commercial was introduced. This used a Spartan Advantage chassis with an American Eagle Series body. Meant as a step between a commercial and a full E-One custom, the super commercial was offered at $137,990 with an MFD-style tilt-cab. The available options were minimal and dealt mainly with accessory items.

This is an E-One Cyclone TC pumper with an XLFDSC cab and a 20-inch vista roof. The rear doors do not extend into the raised roof area, which allows for one long window above the door. It has a rescue-style body with full-height compartments, a 1500-gpm pump, and a 500-gallon water tank. It belongs to the Parkesburg Fire Company Number 1 in Pennsylvania.

At the 1999 Fire Department Instructor's Conference in Indianapolis, E-One introduced the Sentry II pumper series. This product fits between the commercial and custom pumpers in the super commercial category that was already included in the American Eagle product line. The Spartan Advantage cab is built by Marion Body Works of Wisconsin and is available only with an MFDR configuration. The roof has a 10-inch raised section with a full-height door. Spartan added the large E-One grille in place of the small flat grille that is standard with the Advantage. This is an engine-forward, full tilt-cab that uses the Cummins ISC engine with 330- to 350-horsepower. At a glance, the Sentry II cab can be distinguished from a Cyclone II by the side grilles and the side windows, which are level with the base of the windshield. Also, the doors are flush with the cab sides.

Today, the E-One pumper line offers commercial pumpers, Sentry II pumpers, Hush pumpers, Hurricane pumpers, and the Cyclone II pumpers. All custom chassis have standard ABS, multiple cab configurations, and full-height doors that correspond with the vista roof designs. The Hush is a rear-engine design with a wide-open cab that can seat up to 10 people. The Hush is also available with a midengine design for aerials. The Hurricane is a cab-forward tilt-cab design with seating up to 7. The Cyclone II is an engine forward tilt-cab design that can seat up to 10 people. The body styles no longer have names.

E-One uses model numbers that correlate to the size of the compartment between the pump panel and the rear wheel well. There are three pumper styles. The C023 has a 23-inch compartment and is equipped with a 500-gallon water tank as standard. The C034 has a 34-inch compartment and a 500-gallon water tank, while the C044 has a 44-inch compartment and a 1,000-gallon water tank. The rescue pumper bodies that have higher and deeper compartments carry the C400 and C401 model numbers. Since E-One is a custom builder, it will modify these compartments

Here is an E-One Sentry pumper with an upgraded trim package, lighting, and lettering. Purchased by West Granville, Pennsylvania, in 1994, this unit has a top-mount control panel, a 1500-gpm pump, and a 1,000-gallon water tank.

and water tanks per the requests of the purchasing department.

KME

KME, of Nesquehoning, Pennsylvania, builds its own chassis, pumpers, tankers, rescues, and aerial devices. When Grumman Emergency Products went out of business, KME bought the rights and designs for the entire Grumman line of aerial products. It fabricates its own cabs in addition to having its own upholstery shop for the interiors. Overall, KME offers roughly 300 cab and chassis configurations with fixed, tilt, contoured, and squared styles. Each has ABS as a standard feature, in addition to a secondary braking system such as engine brakes, driveline retarders, or transmission retarders.

The primary KME chassis is the full tilt-cab Renegade Series. KME is one of the few manufacturers that still offer a square-cab design in addition to the contoured styles. The cab is constructed of aluminum with the following configurations: SFD, MFD, LMFD, LFD, and XLFD. KME offers raised roofs with 8-inch, 12-inch, or 20-inch heights and full-height doors. The 12- and 20-inch designs can be built with windows in the roof extension area. The SFD configuration is also available in stainless steel or galvanneal steel. The Renegade has a center-mounted front grille that is flat against the cab with a grid pattern design.

KME offers a 12-inch forward extension of the raised roof that begins midway over the front seat, giving the driver and officer additional headroom. The Renegade is also offered in low-profile MFD and LFD styles for aerial apparatus.

In 1996, KME introduced the Excel chassis, which is also a full tilt-cab design. It

Philadelphia gave KME a large order for 1500-gpm custom pumpers in 1995. They feature a Renegade MFDR cab with an exposed step, barrier clearance doors, and a streamlined body style.

KME built this pumper in 1993 for the District of Columbia Fire Department. Engine 8 has a Renegade MFD cab, 1500-gpm pump, 750-gallon water tank, 30-gallon foam tank, and a streamlined body style.

is a premium chassis with many options, cab configurations, and the ability to accommodate any of the electronically controlled engines currently available. Like the Renegade, the front grille is flat and has curved corners around the top. Side grilles are rectangular and sit vertically under the driver's grab rails. This is a contoured cab that is fabricated from aluminum. Cab configurations are SFD, MFD, LMFD, LFD, and XLFD. Unlike the Renegade, raised roof options for the Excel are available in 6-inch, 16-inch, and 22-inch heights. The larger two accommodate windows.

The Excel has largely replaced the Renegade as the primary chassis of choice for KME customers. Renegade models are often specified when a department wants to match other units that are already in its fleet, when it wants a square tilt-cab, or when it prefers the different raised roof options that the Renegade has available.

The Fire Fox and Fire Hawk make up KME's fixed-cab series. The Fire Fox is the

contoured style and the Fire Hawk has a squared cab. Both are cab-forward designs with LFD designs. They are available in aluminum, stainless steel, or galvanneal steel and as two-wheel drive and four-wheel drive models. The Fire Fox is the primary aerial chassis for KME with a low overall height and an available notched roof for nesting aerial devices.

KME builds pumpers with an extruded subframe that is covered with formed panels. It offers aluminum, stainless steel, or galvanneal steel with pumps from all of the major manufacturers, including Hale, Waterous, and Darley. As with most builders, it builds side-mounted, top-mounted, and enclosed interior pump panels. It uses a modular design with a separate pump module to allow for flex. Water tanks can have capacities of up to 3,000 gallons in their pumper/tankers.

KME has several different pumper styles: minipumper, urban interface, wildland, commercial, custom, pumper rescue,

rescue pumper, rear pump, and tanker. They also use square-back, flat-back, and streamline designations that reflect the look of the body. The square back is a traditional body style with a full-width rear tailboard, square compartments, and a beavertail rear panel on each side. The flat-back body is more compact, with flat body panels that extend the full height of the compartments and are flush with the rear tailboard. The streamline style has beavertail compartments with storage space that extends to the tailboard.

The minipumper features a pickup truck chassis with two- or four-wheel drive. It has a 250- or 500-gpm PTO-driven pump, 250-gallon water tank, and an aluminum body.

The urban interface is a midipumper that has a medium-duty commercial chassis. The body can be fabricated from any of the three metals that KME offers and features a 250- to 750-gpm PTO-driven or midship pump. There is a side-mounted operator's panel and a 500 or 750-gallon water tank.

The wildland series features an AM General Hummer chassis. The two-door model can accommodate up to 300 gallons of water, while the four-door model can carry up to 200 gallons. These units feature engine-driven pumps that permit pump-and-roll operations.

Commercial pumpers include the Challenger Series, which features a commercial chassis from Navistar. The IHC 4900 is available with two or four doors, a 1250-gpm pump, 1,000-gallon water tank, and 157-inch flat-back body style in either galvanneal steel or aluminum with limited options. The commercial pumper line provides full custom options, tanks, pumps, and a choice of the three body styles on any commercial chassis. The custom pumper series is the same as the commercial series, with the substitution of a KME custom chassis for the commercial chassis.

The pumper rescue adds deeper, full-height rescue-style compartments to a unit with one of the traditional pumper bodies, while the rescue pumper adds a PTO-driven or midship pump and water tank to a unit with a traditional rescue body.

The rear pump unit offers increased compartment space for rescue and pumper equipment. It also provides for a quieter environment for the pump operator, since he is away from the noise of the engine. This pumper features roll-up doors and places the pump panel at the rear of the unit. The discharge ports are located either on the curb side or driver's side of the unit behind the rear compartment door.

A pumper-tanker is a larger unit with a bigger water tank, larger body, and, often, tandem rear axles.

Pierce

Pierce continues to innovate. In 1992, Pierce continued implementing a program to standardize the front doors on all of its cabs. Prior to this time, the Arrow used a front cab door that featured a straight angled line against the wheel well. The new door is curved around the wheel well and matches the other cabs. The Dash and D-8000 adopted this door in 1990 and the Lance in 1992.

The newer Lance was informally dubbed the Lance 2 to differentiate the wider front door style. The step on the Lance 1 was quite a bit smaller than on the

Overland Park, Kansas, purchased a 1996 All-Steer Pierce Quantum LFD pumper. The rear wheels can be engaged to turn with or against the front wheels in addition to being locked in the forward position. There is a telescoping light tower mounted onto the cab roof of this top-mount 1250-gpm pumper. This unit has a 2G modular body that is apparent from the slight separation between the pump module and the rear body.

Lance 2. For the next year, both styles of Lance cabs were produced, depending on when the order was placed and the projected date of completion. All cabs that utilized the common door had an 11 1/2-inch-deep step that was also 22 inches wide. Another modification that occurred to standardize various aspects of the entire line of cabs, was the implementation of a common front grille. This would be the second grille for the Dash and D-8000 and would match. The Lance was receiving its third grille. The new grilles were as large as the previous Lance grille without the horizontal louvers. The grille had three distinct and equal sections that were separated by a stainless-steel member.

Since all new cabs need to be enclosed, each style had its own available configurations. The Dash was available in an SFD version with rear-facing doors providing seating for six. When the cab was redesigned in 1990 and implemented with the new front doors, grille, and rear-facing doors, the roof over the rear crew area was raised (SFDR) to allow greater access for the firefighters. The available bodies now included low compartments with hard suction hose, high-side compartments, and the newer rescue body to accommodate rescue tools with

full-height and full-depth compartments. The external distinctions separating the Dash and the D-8000 were lost. The only way to tell the difference now was to examine the engine (Detroit Diesel or other optional engine in the Dash; Cummins 6CTAA8 for the D-8000).

When the Pierce Arrow was redesigned with the new doors, it also offered a cab modification to allow a fire department to specify the newer engines with up to 500 horsepower. Here, a low center tunnel was added, resulting in a grille in the center of the cab face. Any engine over 350 horsepower required the tunnel. This grille was smaller and did not match those on the tilt-cab models. The Pierce Arrow has always been a five-person cab with three up front and two in the rear-facing jump seats. But with the tunnel, seating was lost for the third person in the front. Now that all cabs were fully enclosed, the LFD version had forward-facing fold-down seats inside the rear doors to allow seating for a maximum of seven firefighters with the standard cab, or six with the addition of a larger engine and the required tunnel. Although the Pierce Arrow was also available with four-wheel drive, it was only available

with an LFD configured cab with or without the tunnel.

In 1993, Pierce introduced another line of custom chassis. The Saber chassis offered a lower cost full tilt-cab with seating for four, six, or eight. The standard engine offered was the new Detroit Diesel Series 40 with 250 horsepower, but the 300-horsepower version was an available upgrade option. Also standard was the Allison MD3060 five-speed automatic World Transmission. This new engine allowed for the cab design to include a lower doghouse, providing a more open cab interior for improved communication. Limiting the power-train components allowed for economies

in production to keep the cost down. The Saber was introduced in an MFD configuration and was the first Pierce cab that did not utilize a full-length (LFD) rear crew door. Utilizing the same front door and grille as the other tilt-cab models, the rear door that was notched over the wheel well easily distinguished the Saber. Bodies were available in galvanneal steel, aluminum, or stainless steel with custom compartment options to meet the requirements of each fire department.

Also in 1993, the Responder Program was introduced. This program offered a commercial pumper with minimal options to keep costs down and provide faster delivery. The guidelines of the program were based on

The Pierce Quantum chassis features air-operated steps that open and close automatically with the cab doors.

a two- or four-door IHC 4900 Series cab and chassis to streamline production. The Responder Program allowed a selection of water tanks and a choice of 1000- or 1250-gpm Waterous pumps. Side- and top-mounted pump panels were available along with high-side compartments that consisted of two or three separate compartments. Different body lengths allowed for a single- or double-door compartment in front of the rear wheel.

In 1993, Pierce added to the available options for the Dash and D-8000. An LFD version was introduced with full-length rear crew doors on the side of the cab that kept the raised roof over the crew area. Now there were two cab configurations for the Dash and D-8000, the rear-door Dash (SFDR) and the side-door Dash (LFDR). The rear-door Dash offered seating for six, and the side-door Dash had seating for as many as eight. The side-door Dash looked similar to the Lance LFDR but was distinguishable by the solid, full tilt-cab, where the split tilt cab Lance had a seam over the front axle. There

was a third Dash cab style that was made available for rescue squad applications. This version had seating for two with no rear crew area (ER). The roof was flat and the area behind the front axle became a large full-depth storage compartment.

The standard Lance was a six-person LFD split tilt-cab with optional XLFD, XLFDSC, and LFDSC configurations. In 1993, Pierce modified the raised roof options to include a 12-inch extension in addition to the already available 22-inch roof. Both cab heights came with full-height doors for easy egress. The extended cab (XLFD) was available with two different extensions that went beyond the rear door. The first was a 20-inch extension for the Lance 104, and the larger version offered 27 inches for the Lance 104E. The Lance also featured a 45-degree cramp angle for excellent maneuverability.

In 1994, Pierce added Hale pumps to its lineup in addition to the Waterous pumps that it always used. This expanded its customer base to departments that had always used Hale pumps and were reluctant to change. The introduction of the electronic all-wheel steering system, called the ALL STEER for Pierce chassis, came in 1994. The ALL STEER gave the rear axles the ability to turn using three separate steering modes. This effectively reduced a truck's turning radius by one third. The three modes were front-steer, which was the conventional mode; coordinated-steer, in which the rear wheels turn in the opposite direction to the front; and crab-steer, in which all wheels turn the same direction. The coordinated-steer mode gives the tightest turning radius, while the crab-steer mode allows the vehicle to move sideways, providing excellent maneuverability and positioning of the rig.

The Javelin did not prove to be as popular as Pierce had hoped and was no longer offered in 1994 after approximately 100 units had been produced. This year was also the last for the Dash D-8000 chassis.

Also in 1994, Pierce made a major manufacturing change that was implemented throughout its production. Pierce began building modular bodies. Known as the "Second Generation" (2G) body, Pierce would now be able to streamline production and reduce the lead-time for customers. A pumper would now consist of a cab and chassis that was built in one plant, a pump module that was built in another, and a body section that began in yet another area. This would permit all three components to be built at the same time and then assembled into the finished product. Previously, the pump and body sections were built together as a single unit directly onto the chassis, but assembly could not begin until the chassis was completed. Additionally, the new, separate pump house module provided for added structural integrity.

Units throughout 1994 and 1995 were produced with both the first- and second-generation body styles, depending on the specifications and when the unit was ordered. The way to spot the difference between the units is to notice a separation between the area that houses the pump and the rear body. If there is a small gap behind the pump, it is a second-generation body. If the sheet metal above the side-mounted

Pierce introduced the information center in 1998. It is an electronic monitoring system with a digital readout for all of the vehicle's systems including engine conditions, troubleshooting, maintenance items, and safety issues. This display is part of the pump panel. A second display is incorporated into the dashboard on units with a Lance 2000 or Dash 2000 chassis.

pump panel or below the top-mounted pump panel is continuous, then it is the older body style.

In 1995, Pierce made another addition to the Pierce Arrow pumper. Prior to this time, the cab was only available as a standard LFD model. Now it was offered with a 20-inch raised roof and a new MFD style rear door that was notched for the wheel well. Although it extended into the elevated portion of the roof, it did not go the full height. This would be a door that the Pierce Arrow could share with the Saber when Pierce began to offer an MFDR version with a 12-inch raised roof in the same year.

By far, Pierce's grandest announcement in 1995 was the release of its latest top-of-the-line, full-tilt-cab, custom chassis series. Called the Quantum, this cab could seat up to eight firefighters. It was the most unusual and radical cab and chassis introduction in many years. Starting from scratch, Pierce changed the look of fire truck cabs with perhaps the most controversial external design ever built. Gone was the smooth contoured front cab face below the two-piece curved windshield. It was replaced by angled and squared elements that house the headlights and warning lights. These areas surrounded a new grille design that angled toward the front of the cab from the windshield before bending straight down toward the bumper.

In 1997, the fire department of Palm Beach Gardens, Florida, purchased a Pierce Quantum rescue pumper with roll-up doors. The cab configuration was an LFDR that included four colored lights mounted in a vertical line behind the rear cab doors. These four lights correspond to the water tank level indicator lights on the pump panel, allowing the attack crew to monitor its tank water from a distance. This unit also has Pierce's Husky foam system, a 1500-gpm pump, 1,000 gallons of water, and two foam tanks with 20 and 40 gallons.

The one-piece grille had a very open design with bright stainless-steel horizontal members spaced several inches apart, in addition to one piece that went up the center. The radiator was clearly visible through the grille.

The Quantum was designed to provide a maximum of interior space with more headroom and legroom than any other cab. Windows at the top of each door were curved into the roofline, helping to create a more spacious environment. Allowing for easy access and egress from the cab, each door was equipped with air-actuated folding steps that released whenever the door opened and then retracted to a flush position after the door closed. The new steps extend beyond the width of the cab when open and tuck in below the floor level when closed. This translated into an interior cab floor area that was larger than other cabs with traditional steps notched into the floors. The roof was raised 7 inches over other models and the floor was raised 5 inches to almost 4 feet off the ground. Instead of the industry standard of 30 to 36 inches, the engine tunnel in the cab was now only 21 inches from the cab floor, adding to the open interior space for the crew. The engine was also pushed slightly forward, which is why the radiator protruded through the cab, as opposed to being flat like other models.

The standard engine for the Quantum was the Detroit Diesel Series 60 with a range of 350 to 470 horsepower. The Quantum came standard with a 45-degree cramp angle, ABS, and reengineered steering and suspension components for a better ride and superior maneuverability. There were two cab configurations available. The SFD with rear-facing doors allowed seating for six. The LFD style with side doors offered seating for up to eight. As with any chassis, the Quantum would accommodate any custom-designed body style in aluminum, galvanneal steel, or stainless steel.

In 1996, when Pierce was purchased by Oshkosh trucks, it introduced the Husky Foam System, and expanded the Saber line even further. A new 22-inch raised roof became available that could accommodate an enclosed top-mount pump panel. To keep the costs down, this new version used the same height door as the cab with a 12-inch roof extension. Cab configurations for the

Saber consisted of the MFD, MFDR, and the MFDSC styles. The Saber also came with more engine choices, with options from Detroit Diesel and now Cummins providing up to 330 horsepower. In lieu of two of the forward-facing seats along the back wall of the cab, fire departments could now also specify an EMS storage cabinet with a roll-up door. Storage for medical supplies would be more secure inside the cab than in an outside compartment.

The Quantum's popularity was apparent in 1996 with many fire departments placing orders for the new design. A new feature for the Quantum was a raised roof option on the side-door model that was immediately embraced by customers. The rear door with the raised roof configuration was extended and became a full-height door. The roof options included 12-inch and 22-inch extensions for LFDR and LFDSC styles. As the Quantum entered into production, there were a few changes made to the prototype model. The large, open grille was modified into two flat pieces that were recessed slightly. The grille material was much tighter with a mesh design that enhanced the cab's appearance from the front. The radiator was no longer visible from the front without going right up to the grille. The headlight housings were also reconfigured slightly with a more attractive design. Seating configurations now included a maximum of 10 firefighters in the LFD model.

Later in 1996, Pierce introduced a new body style. The heavy-duty rescue pumper was designed to meet the needs of fire departments that required the capabilities of both a pumper and a heavy rescue in a single unit. The body measured 184 inches long and 102 inches wide and incorporated a water tank that was longer and wider than usual. The tank configuration would lower the overall vehicle height and center of gravity for better stability. Compartments were designed for full depth and height to allow for custom configurations of equipment and supplies. This allowed room for slide-out tool boards, a cascade system, recessed reels for electric, air or hydraulic lines, and rescue tools. Unlike a typical pumper, the heavy-duty rescue pumper stored all of the ground ladders

above the water tank with access from the rear of the unit.

In 1997, the Lance custom chassis series offered more cab configuration options than any other chassis made by Pierce. The cabs with a flat roof were available as the standard LFD model and extended XLFD versions with 10-inch, 20-inch, or 27-inch crew cab extensions. The department could customize seating in these cabs for up to 10 firefighters. In addition to the length options, 12-inch and 22-inch crew cab roof extensions were offered. The 22-inch super command roof allowed for an interior command post, enclosed top-mounted pump panel, or just plenty of extra headroom for the crew's comfort. Pierce would also provide a cab-to-body walk-through design for heavy rescue squads. The Lance could accommodate engines with up to 500 horsepower.

Pierce also released another new product in 1997 called the Hawk Wildland Rapid Response Vehicle (RRV). This unit features a four-wheel drive IHC 4900 Series chassis with engines ranging from 250 to 325 horsepower to provide off-road fire fighting capabilities. The Hawk has a high ground clearance, so it can navigate through tough terrain to reach an off-road fire. It has a front bumper turret with an optional brush guard. The turret has a capacity of up to 300 gpm and is electronically controlled from within the cab. The pumper has pump-and-roll capabilities to discharge water, foam, or compressed air foam while moving. Water storage has a maximum capacity of 850 gallons in addition to enough

In 1995, Pierce upgraded the options for the Arrow cab to include a 20-inch raised roof with an MFD rear door. The first unit with this new design went to the O.W.L. VFC of Woodbridge, Virginia. This unit has a 1500-gpm pump, 650 gallons of water, and two 70-gallon foam tanks.

Although Seagrave produces custom chassis for its own products, Seagrave dealers can purchase these chassis for noncompeting units. The Upper Marlboro VFC in Prince Georges County, Maryland, had Marion Body Works fabricate the rescue-style body for this pumper that was not available from Seagrave in 1994. The cab and chassis are an XLFDSC TC50DA with an interior control console and custom crosslays cut into the cab.

foam storage to provide results comparable to the discharge of 6,000 gallons of water. The Hawk can be equipped with PTO-driven or engine-controlled pumps with capacities from 300 to 1000 gpm. The engine-driven pump is controlled by a separate diesel engine mounted in a compartment.

In anticipation of the new millennium, Pierce upgraded the Lance and Dash Series with the Lance 2000 and Dash 2000. Both offer the Pierce Information Center with a console on the dashboard as well as the pump panel. With a digital readout, all functions of the vehicle can be monitored including trouble shooting, maintenance, engine conditions, and safety concerns.

The Dash 2000 boasts a quieter and more open interior. The engine tunnel was lowered 8 inches, the cross tunnel was removed, and a new curved dashboard was added to make all of the controls, switches, and gauges even more accessible than in previous models. The Dash 2000 can be ordered with four-wheel drive, and the cab configurations include an MFD, MFDR (12- and 18-inch raised roof), and MFDSC (24-inch raised roof), with seating for six, seven, or as many as eight. For maneuverability, the chassis has a 45-degree cramp angle and is available with Pierce's electronic all-wheel steering system. The available engines include Cummins, Caterpillar, or Detroit Diesel with up to 500 horsepower, with Allison MD or HD Series transmissions. The Lance 2000 shares all the same upgrades that were incorporated into the Dash 2000.

Currently, Pierce offers the following custom chassis models: the Saber, Dash, Lance, Arrow, and Quantum. The company also produces the Sizzler, Competitor, Responder, and Suburban, which utilize commercial chassis. The Sizzler and Competitor Series are for stripped down stock pumpers, produced in a separate manufacturing facilty in Florida. These units offer few options or upgrades for pre-engineered commercial pumpers.

Seagrave

During the 1990s, Seagrave was the only custom fire truck builder that did not offer its products built on mass-produced commercial chassis. In 1998, it introduced a line of pumpers that are available on the Freightliner Business Class chassis.

Shortly after Seagrave widened its cabs from the industry standard 86 inches to 94 inches, it introduced them as the Commander series. The fixed-cab series carried the model name of the Commander II starting in 1987. This was the beginning of the full-length front doors for Seagrave, although the cabs were still called the H-Series. A four-door version, offered as an option, also had full-length rear doors.

Today, the Commander II cab is the J-Series. These are only offered in the LFD configuration and feature full-length rear doors, unlike pumpers from other companies that utilize MFD rear doors. One available option for these cabs originated with orders for departments in southern California. These departments required short doors with an exposed step. Although this might seem like a throwback to the earlier designs, these doors allow a driver to pull close to the cement barrier wall or guardrail on a highway and still permit the firefighters to swing the doors open so they can get out of the vehicle. Narrow mountain roads with steep hills also hamper full-length doors from easily swinging open. In response to this, some people have informally dubbed these doors "California-style doors."

The Commander II uses a Detroit Diesel or Cummins engine with an Allison automatic transmission as standard. The cabs are all steel reinforced. Seagrave built bodies from galvanneal steel or stainless

steel until 1995, when it added aluminum to the offerings. Seagrave offers both the traditional side pump panel and the top-mount controls finished in stainless steel.

In 1989, Seagrave expanded its custom pumper offerings with the introduction of the Marauder, a tilt-cab design. Depending on the cab configuration, the Marauder is either a full or split tilt-cab. The full tilt-cab accommodates up to 6 people, while the larger cabs with a capacity of up to 10 people split over the front axle. For departments with lower fire station ceilings, the 6-man cab is also available as a split tilt-cab, requiring almost four feet less height for tilting. For safety, Seagrave uses a wired remote control to activate the tilting of the cab. The Marauder has two front grilles. One is square and sits directly in the middle of the cab face and the second, which is roughly half the size of the first, sits just below.

The Marauder offers a true LFD version with a full rear door, LFDSC, XLFD, and XLFDSC. Unlike most other companies, Seagrave does not offer an SFD, an MFD, or a 10-inch raised roof. All cab roofs are either flat or incorporate a full 20-inch raised section. The name Marauder was never used extensively to describe these

units. Instead, the model number designation has always been more common.

Seagrave assigns each unit a six-character identifier. The first character describes the cab as either fixed (J), tilt (T), low profile (L) or commercial (C). The second character signifies the type of vehicle as outlined in Table 2. The third figure describes the pump capacity, while the fourth describes the type of aerial device. The fifth and sixth characters combined identify the engine type and series. The configuration of the cab is not included in this model number.

To accommodate larger engines, Seagrave modified the Commander II cabs in 1993 with a tunnel and front grille. The tunnel allowed for increased cooling for the larger engines such as the Detroit Series 60 and the Cummins N14. At the same time, the J-Cab was offered in an extended version (XLFD). The easiest way to visually differentiate these new J-Cabs from the Marauder tilt-cab series is by the lack of a smaller additional grille below the main grille.

Seagrave fabricates its custom bodies from galvanneal steel or stainless steel. In 1998, Seagrave extended the J-Series and L-Series cabs by 8 inches. Currently, this is the standard and only way to order these cabs.

The Carlisle Fire Company of Milford, Delaware, runs this 1997 1500-gpm Seagrave pumper. This unit has an XLFD TB50DA split tilt-cab with a flat roof and a rescue-style body design.

This is a 1997 Sutphen 2000 Series extruded aluminum rescue pumper for Dayton, Kentucky. It has an MFD custom Sutphen tilt-cab and Sutphen's new rescue pumper body.

Seagrave is currently the exclusive supplier of pumpers and aerial ladders for the FDNY. The balance of the aerials that the FDNY purchases are built on Seagrave chassis. Until recently, Seagrave also was the pumper supplier for the Los Angeles City Fire Department.

Sutphen

Sutphen claims to be the largest of the small custom fire truck manufacturers, and in 1994 it added two tilt-cab models to its custom chassis line. Sutphen was never big on assigning model names or numbers to its chassis, so they will be referred to here with standard designations. Sutphen introduced a full tilt-cab and split tilt-cab version. These cabs can be configured for seating to accommodate from 5 to 10 persons. Options include MFD, LFD, XLFD, R (10-inch raised roof), and SC (super command with a 20-inch raised roof) configurations. Unlike the companies that only build chassis, Sutphen

TABLE 2

Digit	1 Cab	2 Vehicle Type	3 Pump Capacity	4 Type of Arial	5+6 Engine Type and Series
	J=fixed	B=pumper, 4x2	3=1,000 gpm	1=snorkel	CB=Cummins 6C-8.3 liter
	T=tilt	C=chassis only, 4x2	4=1,250 gpm	2=105-foot tower	CN=N-14
	L=low profile	D=pumper, 4x4	5=1,500 gpm	4=75-foot Patriot	DA=Detroit Series 60
	C=commercial	E=pumper tanker, 6x4	6=1,750 gpm	with 500-lb. tip load	DD=Detroit Series 50
		F=chassis only, 4x4	7=2,000 gpm	5=100-foot Patriot	DC=Detroit Series 40
		G=chassis only, 6x4	8=2,250 gpm	with 500-lb. tip load	DH=Detroit 8V92TA
		H=chassis only, 6x6	9=booster pump	6=100-foot Patriot	DF=Detroit 6V92TA
		J=pumper tanker, 6x6	0=no pump	with 250-lb. tip load	
		P=rear mount aerial, 6x4		9=110 foot	
		R=rear mount aerial, 4x2		0=no aerial	
		T=tractor trailer, 4x2			
		X=tractor only, 4x2			

offers a full-length, true LFD model. Its MFD style has a unique attribute. The rear doors come from the same mold as the front doors. These doors have a window that is angled like the front door, but the door is installed in the opposite direction. Since the hinge must be attached to a straight edge, the rear door looks like a mirror image of the front door. The XLFD option has an extension that extends beyond the full-length rear door. Raised roof options are only available with the full-length rear door. Sutphen also offers a full line of fixed-cabs with SFD, MFD, or LFD configurations.

Extruded aluminum pumper bodies are available as well as 12-gauge galvanneal steel, or stainless-steel bodies with custom compartmentation and the choice of top-mounted or side-mounted pump panels.

In 1998, Sutphen introduced its latest pumper series—the Sutphen 2000 Series

extruded aluminum rescue pumper with a custom-built chassis and body. This pumper offers tall compartments that are 28 inches deep to accommodate rescue equipment and tools in addition to traditional pumper gear. With the changing demographics and responses that most fire departments are facing, the rescue pumper has become an extremely viable product.

One of the cabs offered for the Sutphen 2000 Series is a full MFD tilt-cab with new rear doors. This true MFD rear door is straight on both sides, except for the notch for the wheel well. Sutphen also offers a complete array of options with the new and older rear door styles, as well as a choice of full or split tilt-cabs. Sutphen has always prided itself on the simple and practical layout of its operator's panels, as well as the attractive trim packages that are characteristic of each Sutphen pumper.

Copper Mountain, Colorado, took delivery of this 1998 custom Sutphen pumper at the Fire Rescue International Convention in Louisville. Aside from the interesting copper color, this engine has roll-up doors and Sutphen's compact top/side mount operator's control panel.

CHAPTER 6
Pumpers for the Future

The challenges facing fire departments around the country will continue to expand and diversify in the twenty-first century. Two manufacturers, E-One and Pierce, are already designing machines to meet this new age of demands.

E-One

In 1997, E-One unveiled the prototype of a pumper for the new millennium. The Concept 2000 was produced through an alliance with General Electric, Spartech Corporation, and Thermoform Plastics. It is an aerodynamic vehicle that is made of a composite polymer called Millennium III. This futuristic vehicle looks like no other. It features a completely new cab style and a body with everything concealed behind roll-up doors.

In 1998, the Concept 2000 became the Daytona Series. The Daytona is a full MFD tilt-cab that is powered by a Cummins engine and an Allison MD Series automatic transmission. The unit has a 155-inch wheelbase with a 45-degree cramp angle.

E-One built the Daytona Rescue Pumper using a new cab and chassis design, along with a new composite polymer product called Millennium III. It is lightweight, has excellent paint adhesion qualities, and is resistant to damage. *E-One*

Above and below: The light weight aluminum/composite cab shell of the Daytona makes it 20 percent lighter than conventional pumpers. It also resists corrosion. *E-One*

FIRE-RESCUE UNIT

DIAL 911

97

FIRE FIRE

IGNITION
copyright 1997

Unlike other fire trucks, the front door on the Daytona hinges on the "B" post as opposed to the "A" post. This means that it opens in the opposite direction from the rear door. The cab shell is made of high-strength aluminum, and the Millennium III outer skin "is a triple-layer high-performance composite polymer extrusion." It is resistant to damage and still lightweight. E-One estimates a 20 percent weight reduction over conventional pumpers. In addition, when painted, the automotive-like finish will not corrode.

The cab interior provides a wraparound dashboard and the addition of several controls incorporated into the center of the steering wheel. The cab can be configured to seat up to eight firefighters. The Daytona offers Hale or Waterous pumps that can be mounted midship or in the rear. Midship pumps can deliver 1000 or 1250 gpm, while a rear pump can go up to 1500 gpm. In either position, the control panel is recessed within a compartment. All of the gauges are fully electronic, which eliminates the additional wires and connections necessary with analog gauges. The compartments

have optional steps that fold down to allow easier access to the top areas of the full-height compartments.

The Daytona Series entered into production in January 1999.

Pierce

Pierce took a different approach in designing its next-generation pumper. Pierce decided to produce its concept in the form of a one-eighth—scale model in hopes of gaining feedback from fire service professionals, before going through the expense of tooling up for actual production.

The new design is called the First Response Vehicle (FRV). This unit combines the capabilities of an ambulance and a pumper on a custom chassis apparatus that is smaller than many of the big rigs produced today.

Due to the reduction of fires nationwide, Pierce wants to produce a vehicle that better addresses the types of calls to which fire departments must respond. More and more, fire departments are called on for nonfire emergencies. Calls for EMS and motor vehicle accidents have become the

Class 1 combined many of the desirable attributes for a future fire engine into this artist's conceptual drawing. *Class 1*

An artist's rendering of Pierce's FRV concept vehicle illustrates the futuristic cab and chassis design along with the integral rescue body. *Pierce Manufacturing*

majority of the day-to-day activities for many fire departments.

The FRV is based on a short wheelbase of 140 to 150 inches and will be less expensive than a conventional pumper. It will be capable of making an initial attack on a fire, while providing a full-size ambulance for patient care and transport. Instead of sending an ambulance or medic unit with a full-size engine company as backup, the FRV will put a full engine company on-scene without the need for the additional unit.

The preliminary specifications for the FRV include a four-door cab with seating for five. The fire/EMS unit will have a full-service ambulance body with external rescue compartments, a 300-gallon water tank, fire pump, attack and supply hose, and ground ladders in a separate module between the cab and ambulance body. The fire unit will have a 500-gallon water tank, fire pump, hose, ladders, and larger compartments. A 275-horsepower

engine will power the FRV. The basic vehicle design, which includes its own custom chassis, will offer five options for the FRV. Basic designs will offer a pumper for fire fighting only, an ambulance unit for patient care and transport, or a unit combining fire fighting with patient care and transport. Other variations will include a rescue squad, or a specialty unit for mobile command and communications. Each configuration will take advantage of the short wheelbase, economical pricing, and excellent maneuverability.

The FRV is a multipurpose vehicle that can provide fire suppression and EMS capabilities from the same unit on a new custom chassis.

Pierce and E-One have released these designs, representing the next generation of fire trucks. Undoubtedly, others in the industry are in the research and design stage for their own apparatus applications to carry them into the next millennium.

3D Fire Apparatus, 89, 95, 104
4 Guys, Inc., 13, 96, 97
Advanced life support (ALS), 83
Alexis Fire Equipment, 13, 86, 96
Allison, 88, 90, 93, 95, 101, 105, 106, 113, 118, 123
Alsip (IL) Fire Department, 44
American Eagle, 13, 20, 49, 107
American LaFrance, 9, 11, 13, 24–26, 49, 58, 95, 101–104
    700 Series, 24
    ALF-123, 104
    ALF-123R, 104
    ALF-134, 103
    ALF-135, 104
    ALF-135R, 104
    ALF-148, 103
    Business Class Series, 101
    Century 2000 Series, 26
    Century Series, 25
    Century Straightline, 25
    Challenger Series, 25
    Commercial Pumper Series, 25
    Commodore Series, 25
    Eagle Series, 102, 103
    Metropolitan, 104
    Pacemaker Series, 21, 26
    Patriot Series, 26
    Pioneer III, 28
    Pioneer Series, 25, 77, 82
Anaheim (CA) Fire Department, 94
Attack crew, 76
Attack line, 76, 79, 80, 82
Auke Bay (AK) Fire Department, 17, 18
Baltimore (MD) Fire Department, 44
Baltimore County (MD) Fire Department, 98
Basic life support (BLS), 83
Batavia (IL) Fire Department, 9
Boardman, 13, 14, 16, 21, 49
Bodies, design, 58–62
Booster line, 68
Borrego Springs (CA) Fire Department, 51
Boyer, 13, 49
Brentwood (PA) Fire Department, 21
Cabs, design, 56–58
Carlisle (Milford, DE) Fire Company, 119
Caterpillar, 53, 55, 90, 93, 103, 104, 118
Central States Fire Apparatus, 59, 88, 96
    Centurion Lite, 96
    Centurion, 96
Chassis, design, 51–53
Chemical Hook and Ladder Company (Colonia, NJ), 105
Cherry Valley (IL) Fire Department, 100
Chevrolet, 41, 42
    K-30, 34
Chicago (IL) Fire Department, 30, 71, 75, 78, 80, 90, 98
Cincinnati Cab, 14
Clinton (MD) Fire Department, 36
Cockeysville (MD) Fire Department, 97
Compressed Air Foam System (CAFS), 69
Copper Mountain (CO) Fire Department, 121
Crown Firecoach Company, 11, 13, 31, 49

Cummins, 53, 55, 88–90, 94, 95, 97, 99, 101, 103–105, 108, 112, 117–119, 123
Darley, 13, 16, 23, 40–42, 77, 93, 95, 96, 110
    Challenger S750, 41
    Challenger Series, 40, 42
    Champion, 41
    Engager Series, 41, 42
    Monarch Series, 41, 42
    Patriot, 42
    RF750, 41
Dayton (KY) Fire Department, 120
Delaware Engine Company (Port Jervis, NY), 22
Detroit Diesel, 53, 54, 88, 89, 95, 97, 103–105, 112, 113, 116, 118, 119
District of Columbia Fire Department, 110
Dodge, 41
    W-400, 34
Driver, 71, 73, 74, 79, 80
Duplex, 11, 14–16, 28, 48, 100
    D-250, 14
    D-250-T, 14
    D-260 Liberty, 14
    D-300-FD, 14
    D-300-LP, 14
    D-350 Enforcer, 14
    D-400, 14
    D-450 Defender, 14
    D8400, 16
    D9400 Signature, 15
    D9400L, 16
    D9400M, 16
    D9400R, 16
    D9400X, 16
    D9500 Signature, 15, 16
    R-200, 14
    R-300, 14
East Sunbury (PA) Hose Company, 20
Eaton Fuller, 53
Elkins Park Volunteer (Cheltenham Township, PA), Fire Company, 35
Emergency Medical Technician (EMT), 83
Emergency One, 13, 16, 26–33, 49, 58, 59, 66, 100, 104–108, 123, 125
    15060 Quick Attack Rescue Pumper, 26
    20084 Quick Attack Rescue Pumper, 27, 32
    20102 Quick Attack Rescue Pumper, 32
    C023, 108
    C034, 108
    C044, 108
    C400, 108
    C401, 108
    Class 1, 124, 125
    Concept 2000, 123
    Cyclone II, 107, 108
    Cyclone TC, 32, 33, 105–107
    Cyclone, 30–33, 105, 107
    Daytona Rescue Pumper, 123
    Daytona Series, 123, 125
    Guardsman Series, 27, 29
    Hurricane TC, 106
    Hurricane, 29–31, 32, 78, 105, 107, 108
    Hush EMS Series, 106
    Hush Vista, 32
    Hush XL, 31

    Hush, 29, 30, 32, 105, 108
    Protector I TM, 29
    Protector I, 28, 29
    Protector II, 28, 29
    Protector III, 28, 29
    Protector IV, 28, 29
    Protector Series, 28
    Protector TC, 33
    Protector XL Series, 31
    Protector XLT, 31
    Protector, 32, 104, 106, 107
    Sentry I, 27, 29
    Sentry II, 108
    Sentry III TM, 29
    Sentry III, 27, 29, 75
    Sentry IV, 29
    Sentry Series, 27, 29
    Sentry, 80, 104, 105, 107
    Series 10060, 26
    Tower Ladder, 75
    Town and Country, 32
Emergency Vehicle Team, 99
Emerson (NY) Fire Department, 101
EMS, 83
Equipment placement, 68
Equipment storage, 68
Federal Motors, 29
Federal Signal Corporation, 100
Fellowship (Mount Laurel, NJ) Fire Company, 46
Ferrara Fire Apparatus (FFA), 13, 59, 86, 96, 97
    Inferno, 97
    Intruder, 97
Fire Rescue Group, 100
FMC, 13, 16, 21, 23, 42–45, 49, 65
    Commander, 44, 45
    Commercial Firefighters, 42
    Custom Firefighters, 42
    Omega Series, 43–45
    Quick-Attack Pumper Series, 43
    Ram Series, 43
    Roughneck, 42
    Semi-Custom, 42
    Sentinel Series, 44, 45
    Van Pelt Series, 44, 45
Fog nozzle, 76, 82
Ford, 11, 41, 42, 46, 51, 104, 107
    C Series, 11, 35, 43, 67, 75, 80
    C-8000, 38, 45
    C900, 77
    F-350, 34
Forward lay, 72, 80
Freightliner, 51, 95, 97, 98, 101, 102, 104
    American LaFrance, 101
    Business Class FL-106, 101
    Business Class FL-112, 101, 102
    Business Class FL-50, 101
    Business Class FL-60, 101
    Business Class FL-70, 101
    Business Class FL-80, 98, 99, 101, 102

    Business Class Series, 39
Frontline, 23
Fuller Ceemat, 90
Fuller, 53
FWD, 9–11
Gator, 21
General Electric, 123
General Motors, 41, 51
GMC/White, 104
Gobles Pine Grove (MI) Fire Department, 87
Godiva, 104
Great Falls (MT) Fire Department, 98
Greensboro (NC) Fire Department, 14
Grumman, 13, 16–18, 23, 45–47, 49, 85, 95, 109
    Attackcat, 46, 47
    Customcat, 46
    Firecat, 46, 47
    Minicat, 46, 47
    Panther Series, 46
    Tankercat, 46
    Tigercat, 46
    Wildcat, 46
Haddon (Haddonfield, NJ) Fire Company, 26
Hahn, 11, 13, 47–49
    HCP Series, 48
    Jetcoat, 47
Hale, 96, 99, 104, 110, 114, 125
Haverhill (MA) Fire Department, 89
Hendrickson, 11, 14, 16, 17, 28, 46, 48
    1871, 41
    1871-C, 14, 16, 17
    1871-S, 16, 17, 36
    1871-W, 14, 17
    1871-WS, 18
    1871-WT, 17
    VT-100, 86
Herrin (IL) Fire Department, 17
HME, 17, 18, 26, 58, 71, 85–90, 96, 99, 100
    1871 Series, 85, 87, 89
    1871 SFO Series, 87, 88
    1871-P Series, 86, 87, 89, 97
    1871-P2 Series, 88
    Classic Series, 85
    Intruder, 86
    Panther Series, 17
    SFO, 90, 98
    SFO-Lite Series, 88, 96
    VT-Fire, 86
Hose man, 74
Howe, 16, 45, 49
Husky Foam System 116
Hydrant man, 79
Imperial, 11, 14, 18
Indiana Fire Apparatus, 13
International, 11, 32, 41, 51, 107, 117, 4900 Series, 39
Javelin, 37
Kent (WA) Fire Department, 54
Kenworth, 51

KME, 13, 58, 109–111
    AM General Hummer, 111
    Challenger Series, 111
    Excel Series, 109, 110
    Fire Fox, 110
    Fire Hawk, 110
    Renegade Series, 109, 110
Kovatch Mobile Equipment (KME), 17
Ladder Towers, Inc. (LTI), 16, 104
Lederle Labs (Pearl River, NY) Fire Brigade, 19
Long Beach (CA) Fire Department, 114
Los Angeles (CA) Fire Department, 31, 80
Luverne, 59, 78, 95, 98, 99
    Commander II, 99
    Commander III, 99
    Commander IV, 99
    Commander Models I, 98
    Commando, 99
    Lear Series, 99
    Legend Series, 99
    Tradition Series, 99
    TSS, 99
    XL Series, 99
Mack L Model, 11
Mack, 9, 11, 13, 17, 33, 34, 49
    B Model, 11
    C-85, 33
    C-95, 33
    C-Series, 33
    CF Series, 33, 34
    MC Series, 32, 34
    MS Series, 34
    R Series, 34
    Renault, 34
Marion Body Works of Wisconsin, 108, 118
Master stream, 68
Maxim, 11, 13
Meritor, 53
Millennium III, 123, 125
Morton Grove (IL) Fire Department, 10
National Fire Protection Association (NFPA), 20
National Foam, 14, 19
National Institute of Health (Bethesda, MD), 49
Navistar, 101, 104, 111
New Midway (MD) Volunteer Fire Company, 103
New York (NY) Fire Department, 25, 34, 48, 120
Nolan Company, 14
Nozzle man, 83
O.W.L. (Woodbridge, VA) Fire Company, 106, 117
Oak Park (IL) Fire Department, 23
Oren, 45
Oshkosh, 14, 36, 116
Overland Park (KS) Fire Department, 111
Palm Beach Gardens (FL) Fire Department, 37, 116
Parkesburg (PA) Fire Department, 107
Patton Bridgeton Terrace (MO) Fire Protection District, 39
Pemfab, 14, 18–22, 28, 46, 48
    93 Cab, 18
    932-S, 18
    932-T, 18
    934-S, 18

934-T, 18
Imperial T942, 20
Imperial T962 Series, 20
Imperial T964 Series, 21
Imperial, 20
Marquis, 20
Maxi 942, 18
Maxi 944, 18
Premier, 19
Royale, 19, 20
S-932, 19
S-934, 19
S-942, 19
S-944, 19
Sentinel, 21
SLP-942, 19
SLP-944, 19
Sovereign, 19
T-942+2, 19
T-942+4, 19
T-942+8, 19
T-942, 19
T964 Series, 20
Wedge 932-T, 19
Wedge, 18
Peterbilt, 51, 104
Philadelphia (PA) Fire Department, 109
Pierce, 13, 16, 34–39, 58, 67, 95, 111–118, 125, 126
    Arrow, 35–37, 73, 112, 114
    Competitor, 118
    D-8000, 111, 114
    Dash 2000, 68, 118
    Dash, 37, 38, 59, 111, 112, 114
    Fire Marshal, 34, 36
    First Response Vehicle (FRV), 125, 126
    Hawk Wildland Rapid Response Vehicle (RRV), 117
    HD Suburban, 34, 36
    Javelin, 39, 115
    Lance 104, 114
    Lance 104E, 114
    Lance 2, 111
    Lance 2000, 118
    Lance, 38, 54, 111, 114, 117
    Minuteman, 34, 35
    Quantum, 111, 113, 115–117
    Responder Program, 113
    Responder, 118
    Saber, 74, 112, 113, 116, 117
    Second Generation (2G), 115
    Sizzler, 118
    Suburban 1000, 34, 35
    Suburban 750, 34, 35
    Suburban, 39, 118
Pirsch, 9–11, 13, 14, 16, 48, 49
    Five-man deluxe canopy cab, 48
Pittsfield (MA) Fire Department, 93
Plymouth (PA) Fire Company, 47
Ponderosa (Houston, TX) Volunteer Fire Department, 112
Power Plants, design, 53–56

Pump operator, 72, 73, 76, 79
Pumps, design, 62–67
Quality, 13, 95, 99, 100
    Avenger, 99
RD Murray, 101, 104
Reverse lay, 73, 79, 90
Road Rescue, 95
Rockwell, 53
San Francisco (CA) Fire Department, 95
Saulsbury, 12, 24, 65, 94, 100
    J-Series, 100
    Stealth Pumper Series, 94, 100
Scene lighting, 67
Seagrave, 9, 11, 13, 39, 40, 52, 58, 63, 95, 118–120
    531-B, 11
    B Series, 11, 83
    Commander II, 118, 119
    H-Series, 40, 118
    HB Series, 74
    Invader Series, 40
    J-Cab, 119
    J-Series, 118
    L-Series, 119
    Marauder, 119
    P-Series, 38, 39
    PB-Series, 39, 40
    SR-Series, 39
    TB50DA, 119
    TB60DA, 76
    TC50DA, 118
    W-Cab, 40
    WB Series, 39
Shrewesbury (PA) Fire Company, 13
Simon, 15
Simon-Duplex, 15, 43
    D500 Vanguard, 15, 17
    D8400 Classic, 15, 16
    Mark II, 15, 16
Smeal Fire Apparatus Company, 87, 100, 101
    Watchdog Series, 87, 100
Smooth-bore nozzle, 82
Southboro (MA) Fire Department, 88
Spartan, 14, 22–24, 28, 41, 42, 44, 46, 48, 51, 90–96, 99, 100
    Advantage, 95, 99, 107, 108
    Baron, 90–92, 94
    CFC Supercab, 22
    CFG Model, 14
    CFG SpaceMaster, 22
    CFV Maxi-Vision, 22
    CFV, 14
    Charger, 90–92, 94
    Diamond, 78, 90–92, 98
    Eurospace, 24
    FA20, 24
    FC20, 24
    FS20, 24
    Gladiator Command Cab, 23
    Gladiator Super Command Cab, 23
    Gladiator, 22, 23, 90–92, 95
    GT One, 93

Lifesaver, 24
MA20, 24
Maxi-Vision, 14
MC20, 24
Metro Star, 91, 92, 95
Monarch, 24, 44, 90, 91
MS20, 24
RA20, 23
RS20, 23
Silent Knight, 90–92, 94
Total Response One (TR-1), 94
TR-1, 95
Spartech Corporation, 123
Spencer, 87
Spicer, 53
St. Charles (IL) Fire Department, 41
St. Louis (MO) Fire Department, 72
Steeldraulics, 13
Sutphen, 13, 40, 55, 58, 120, 121
    2000 Series, 120, 121
TCM, 18, 22, 40, 47
    Cincinnati, 48
Thermoform Plastics, 123
Truck Cab Manufacturers (TCM), 14
Union City Body Corp., 99
Upper Marlboro (Prince Georges County, MD) VFC, 118
Van Pelt Fire Truck Company, 13, 44, 49
Volvo, 104
Wading River (NY) Fire Department, 59
Ward '79 Limited, 13, 14, 34, 48, 49
    Apollo Series, 49
    Fire Mac Series, 49
    Fire Max Series, 49
    Jupiter Series, 49
    Mercury Series, 49
    Vulcan Series, 49
Ward LaFrance, 11, 13, 49
    Ambassador Series, 29
Warner Swassey Company, 14
Water supply, 69
Waterous, 96, 99, 110, 114, 125
Watertown (CT) Fire Department, 44
Wayne Township Fire Department, 16
Weirton (WV) Fire Department, 55
West Deptford Township (Thorofare, NJ) Station 61, 15
West Granville (PA) Fire Department, 108
Western States Company, 13, 51
Willing (Montoursville, PA) Hose Company, 43
Wilmette (IL) Fire Department, 38
Winter Park (FL) Fire Department, 28
World War I, 47
World War II, 9, 11, 47
Yonkers (NY) Fire Department, 85
Young Fire Apparatus Company, 13, 16, 49
    Crusader II, 16